AF417950

Grit and Gratitude

THE SCIENCE AND ART OF A SUCCESSFUL CAREER AND LIFE

By Adam Hickman, Ph.D., & LynnAnn Brewer, MAIS

innovativeink
PUBLISHING
A Division of Kendall Hunt

DISCLAIMER: This Author-owned published work created by the author, who is and shall remain solely responsible for its content. The views and opinions expressed in this publication are those of the author/s and do not necessarily reflect the views or positions of Innovative Ink Publishing ("IIP"), Kendall Hunt Publishing Company ("Kendall Hunt") or their parent or affiliated companies, officers, directors or employees. IIP and/or Kendall Hunt have provided limited technical services only to assist the author with the author-owned publication of this work and assume no responsibility or liability for any of author's content, opinions, errors, inaccuracies, omissions, or any other inconsistencies herein and hereby disclaims any liability to any party for any loss, damage or disruption caused by such content, errors, inaccuracies, omission, or any other inconsistencies.

If this publication is fictional, the names, characters, businesses, places and events and incidents in this publication are fictional. Any resemblance to actual persons, living or dead, or actual events or places is purely coincidental.

If this publication is non-fictional, this book and its content are: (i) provided on an "as is" basis, and no representations or warranties of any kind is made by author and/or Kendall Hunt or Innovative Ink with respect to this book or its contents; (ii) for informational purposes only and is not intended to diagnose, treat, remediate, cure, or prevent any condition or disease; and (iii) not intended as a substitute for consultation with a licensed professional, consultant or technician, and it is recommended you consult with your own licensed professional, consultant or technician regarding any suggestions and recommendations made in this book. Neither the author, nor IIP and/or Kendall Hunt assume any responsibility for errors, inaccuracies, omissions, or any other inconsistencies herein.

Cover image © Shutterstock.com

www.innovativeinkpublishing.com
Send all inquiries to:
4050 Westmark Drive
Dubuque, IA 52004-1840

Copyright © 2025 by Adam Hickman and LynnAnn Brewer

Print ISBN: 979-8-3851-5755-6
eBook ISBN: 979-8-3851-5756-3

All rights reserved. No part of this publication may be reproduced,
stored in a retrieval system, or transmitted, in any form or by any means,
electronic, mechanical, photocopying, recording, or otherwise,
without the prior written permission of the copyright owner.

Published in the United States of America

DEDICATION

From LynnAnn: I dedicate this work to my family: my dad, Hien Khac Nguyen, and my mom in heaven, Muoi Tang. I also thank my husband, Danny, sweet children, siblings, and my forever friends and chosen sisters, Chawn and Annie.

From Adam: Ellie, Ben, and Nina – you are my greatest stories. Your laughter, curiosity, and endless love inspire me daily. One day, when you read this, you'll understand why I encourage you to pursue your passions and, as Mom says, to be true to yourselves. Embrace your uniqueness, chase your dreams, and with a bit of grit and gratitude, you'll achieve incredible things in this world. Love always, Dad.

Contents

Prologue

Two universal forces shape our lives, no matter our age, race, gender, or where we call home. These forces reach beyond surface-level differences and tap into the core of what makes life rich and meaningful. In a world full of uncertainty and turbulence, two guiding principles offer a compass: grit and gratitude.

Grit is the inner strength that drives us forward when the road becomes steep and the way unclear. It is the relentless determination to keep moving, even when the odds are stacked against us. Grit is waking up each day with the resolve to pursue your goals, to rise after every fall, to face challenges with courage, and to silence the voice of self-doubt. It is not just about perseverance; it's about pushing through, fueled by purpose.

Gratitude, in contrast, is the quiet practice of being fully present and recognizing the value in what is. It is the lens that helps us see the small triumphs and quiet joys that are often overlooked. Gratitude allows us to find light in the darkest of moments, to embrace the lessons in failure, and to appreciate the beauty hidden within our struggles. It brings peace, offering balance to grit's relentless pursuit.

The world today craves a resurgence of these timeless virtues. As we navigate this era of rapid change and overwhelming challenges, grit and gratitude provide a foundation for resilience and hope. This story is about finding strength in adversity, about forging ahead with unbreakable perseverance while embracing grace in each moment.

In the following chapters, you'll meet individuals who embody these principles. Their stories will inspire, challenge, and encourage you to reflect on your own journey. You will see how the blend of grit and gratitude has transformed their lives, and you may discover new ways to integrate these values into your own.

This book is designed for you to explore as you need, in any order that aligns with your growth in grit and gratitude.

As you dive into this narrative, remember that these aren't just concepts to admire from a distance. Grit and gratitude are tools—powerful ones—to shape your life and guide your way. They are skills to be honed, and perspectives that can redefine how you see the world.

Let this prologue be the start of your own comeback story, where grit empowers you and gratitude grounds you.

Both the workplace and the world are waiting for your impact.

About the Authors

LYNNANN

LynnAnn Nguyen Brewer is an Executive Advisor with over 25 years of HR leadership experience. She has guided HR leaders, from directors to CHROs, on leadership, organizational development, and building impactful workplace cultures. Her insights on HR and diversity have been featured in Fortune, Essence, and Yahoo. As a co-author of *Grit and Gratitude*, she shares lessons from her personal and professional journey.

Born into a Vietnamese war refugee family and a first-generation college graduate, LynnAnn's background shapes her commitment to diversity, equity, and inclusion. Her work has contributed to organizations being recognized as top employers for women, veterans, and diversity.

Outside of work, LynnAnn is a dedicated mom, wife, and eldest sister of five. She volunteers with the Texas Women's Conference, advocating for women's equity and mentoring others. Her early experiences overcoming cultural and economic challenges fuel her passion for supporting underrepresented voices.

ADAM

Adam Hickman, Ph.D., is an accomplished expert in organizational development, leadership, and employee engagement. With over a decade of experience in the field, Hickman has built a reputation for his innovative approaches to workplace dynamics and his deep understanding of what drives employee motivation. His career spans various roles, from consulting and coaching to research and leadership development.

He holds advanced degrees in business and organizational leadership, combining academic rigor with practical, real-world insights. Hickman is best known for his work with Gallup, where he has helped numerous organizations enhance productivity, foster employee engagement, and improve leadership practices through data-driven strategies.

Hickman is also a thought leader who regularly contributes to discussions on employee well-being, remote work, and the evolving nature of leadership. His expertise has made him a sought-after speaker and writer, providing actionable insights for leaders who wish to create thriving, high-performing teams. With a focus on human potential and business outcomes, Hickman's work continues to influence how organizations develop their people and cultivate more engaged, resilient cultures.

1

Understanding Grit

Grit, as a concept, transcends mere persistence or resilience.

Grit is that inner awakening that pushes you daily.

Defined by psychologist Angela Duckworth, grit encompasses a combination of passion and perseverance toward long-term goals. Unlike fleeting enthusiasm or short-lived determination, grit involves sustained effort and interest over months, years, or even decades. This unique blend of steadfastness and dedication distinguishes it from other traits like resilience, which focuses on bouncing back from setbacks, or motivation, which can wane over time.

Historically, grit has been an implicit part of human achievement long before psychology formally recognized it. Historical figures, such as Thomas Edison, with his relentless pursuit of innovation, or Marie Curie, with her groundbreaking work in radioactivity despite immense personal and professional obstacles, exemplify the essence of grit. These individuals maintained unwavering focus and effort toward their goals, often facing repeated failures and societal pressures.

From a cultural perspective, grit has often been romanticized and celebrated in literature and folklore. Stories of explorers braving the unknown, inventors toiling in obscurity, and leaders persevering through crises have all contributed to a societal admiration for tenacity and hard work. The

American Dream emphasizes achieving success through perseverance and hard work and encapsulates the cultural valorization of grit.

Critical to understanding grit is knowledge of its opposite and contrast. The opposite of grit is giving up, apathy, fragility, timidity, complacency, and helplessness.

THE SCIENCE BEHIND GRIT: PSYCHOLOGICAL AND PHYSIOLOGICAL ASPECTS

Psychologically, grit involves a profound alignment between one's passion and long-term objectives. This alignment fosters intrinsic motivation, which is crucial for maintaining sustained effort. According to Duckworth, individuals with high levels of grit demonstrate a persistent interest in their goals, coupled with a resilience that allows them to overcome obstacles and setbacks. This psychological steadfastness is supported by goal-setting theories, which emphasize the importance of setting long-term, challenging, yet attainable goals.

Cognitive-behavioral theories also play a role in understanding grit. These theories suggest that individuals with high levels of grit engage in positive self-talk and reframe challenges as opportunities for growth. They are less likely to be discouraged by setbacks and more likely to maintain a positive outlook on their progress and potential.

Physiologically, the brain plays a significant role in fostering grit. The prefrontal cortex, responsible for decision-making and self-control, is particularly active in gritty individuals. This brain region helps regulate emotions, suppress impulses, and maintain focus on long-term objectives, even when faced with immediate temptations or distractions. Additionally, the release of neurotransmitters such as dopamine reinforces reward pathways associated with achieving long-term goals, further sustaining motivation and effort.

Recent neuroscience research has also highlighted the role of neuroplasticity in developing grit. The brain's ability to form and reorganize synaptic connections in response to learning and experience means that individuals can cultivate grit through practice and persistence. This adaptability underscores the importance of sustained effort and the potential for personal growth in the face of challenges.

FAMOUS EXAMPLES OF GRIT IN ACTION

Throughout history and contemporary society, numerous individuals have exemplified grit through their relentless pursuit of excellence and achievement. Consider the stories of J.K. Rowling and Amy Tan, two authors who faced significant obstacles. Rowling, author of the Harry Potter series, faced numerous rejections before finally publishing the first book and struggled with financial hardships and personal struggles. Similarly, Amy Tan, bestselling author of "The Joy Luck Club," was told she'd never make it as a novelist and faced rejection from 12 publishers before her debut novel's eventual publication. Despite these challenges, both women demonstrated unwavering dedication to their writing, highlighting the power of grit. Their stories testify to the transformative impact of perseverance and determination, inspiring countless individuals to pursue their passions and overcome adversity. Through their remarkable journeys, Rowling and Tan show that grit can turn dreams into reality, despite seemingly insurmountable obstacles.

In the realm of sports, David Goggins stands as a testament to grit. Renowned for his extraordinary endurance and mental toughness, Goggins has pushed the boundaries of human potential through feats that seem almost superhuman. His journey vividly illustrates relentless perseverance, from completing multiple ultramarathons and triathlons to setting world records in endurance challenges. Beyond physical accomplishments, Goggins' story of overcoming personal adversities, including a challenging childhood and obesity, underscores the power of sheer determination and mental fortitude. His resilience and unyielding spirit inspire athletes and non-athletes to push through their limitations and strive for greatness.

A STORY OF DR. JOHN JAQUISH

In writing this book, I had the opportunity to interview Dr. John Jaquish, someone whose everyday grit I greatly admire. Dr. Jaquish is an American scientist, author, and entrepreneur known for his groundbreaking work in health and fitness. He is the inventor of the X3 Bar, a portable resistance training system that uses variable resistance to help users build muscle and improve overall fitness and wellness. This system emerged from his research into the biomechanics of bone density—a journey that began with his quest to help his mother, who had been diagnosed with osteoporosis. This research also led to the creation of the bioDensity device, a machine designed to increase bone density, now widely used in medical and fitness facilities worldwide.

Dr. Jaquish is also the author of the book *Weight Lifting is a Waste of Time: So is Cardio, and There's a Better Way to Have the Body You Want*, which challenges traditional fitness paradigms and promotes a new approach to strength training. Beyond his work as an inventor and author, he is a frequent speaker on topics related to exercise science, human performance, and biohacking.

While his inventions and fame are noteworthy, what impresses me most is his sheer determination and mastery of grit. I began following Dr. Jaquish's work in 2020, and after reading *Weight Lifting is a Waste of Time*, I was captivated. The book challenges conventional wisdom around diet and fitness with research and concepts that turn traditional teachings on their head. But his work isn't about seeking fame—it's about fostering grit and putting health and wellness at the forefront.

During my conversations with Dr. Jaquish, it became clear that his dedication to grit is evident in everything he does. His "why" is unmistakable: he invests hundreds of hours teaching, educating, and correcting misconceptions based on data and science. One notable example is his advocacy for the carnivore diet—a stark contrast to the Standard American Diet (S.A.D.). After trying it myself and undergoing regular bloodwork, I saw significant transformations in my body, mental clarity, and overall well-being. This journey would not have been possible without the grit I developed after discovering his book. And it's not just my story; there are thousands of similar stories within the online communities around his X3 program.

What stands out about people with true grit is that they don't rely on motivation—they rely on discipline. Discipline in their purpose, brand, and mission. Dr. Jaquish stays true to his narrative, backing his viewpoints with science and personally engaging with his community. As he once told me, "People follow people, not a brand." I see this in action every week when he responds to those who challenge his ideas, holding firm to his principles with data and evidence.

Dr. Jaquish also mentioned Mark Twain, quoting him to highlight how simple things have been made unnecessarily complex, often due to profit motives. When I asked him how he measures success, it was clear he has an extreme sense of clarity on the topic. As Aristotle said, "Where your talents and the needs of the world cross, there lies your vocation." Dr. Jaquish is living his vocation, right where he is, doing what he does. His vision of success lies in seeing others experience the same awakening I did—when variable resistance becomes the global standard over traditional weights, and when his research's benefits are normalized across all areas of fitness, leading us to stop wasting time on outdated fitness methods and instead focus on building strength and improving our diets for genuine well-being.

In science, Jane Goodall's lifelong dedication to studying and preserving primates in their natural habitats showcases grit in the face of environmental challenges and scientific skepticism. Her passion for her work and perseverance in the field have led to groundbreaking discoveries and significant contributions to conservation efforts. Goodall's commitment to her research, often conducted under harsh and isolating conditions, demonstrates the role of sustained passion and perseverance in achieving long-term goals.

Howard Schultz's journey with Starbucks illustrates grit in action in the business world. Coming from a modest background, Schultz faced numerous challenges in transforming Starbucks from a small coffee bean retailer into a global coffeehouse chain. His vision, coupled with relentless effort and resilience in the face of setbacks, showcases how grit can drive entrepreneurial success.

Malala Yousafzai's life is a testament to the power of grit and determination. Born in Swat Valley, Pakistan, Malala defied the Taliban's ban on girls' education, speaking out publicly for her right to learn. In 2012, she survived a brutal assassination attempt by the Taliban, who shot her in the head. Miraculously, Malala recovered and continued to advocate for girls' education, becoming the youngest Nobel Prize laureate in 2014. Her unwavering courage and resilience in the face of violence and oppression have inspired millions worldwide, and her nonprofit, the Malala Fund, continues to fight for every girl's right to 12 years of free, safe, and quality education. Through her remarkable journey, Malala has shown that even in the darkest of times, grit and determination can lead to extraordinary achievements.

ASSESSING YOUR LEVEL OF GRIT

Understanding and developing grit within oneself begins with self-assessment. Duckworth's Grit Scale is a valuable tool for measuring an individual's level of grit. This scale evaluates two main components: consistency of interests and perseverance of effort. By honestly answering questions about one's long-term goals, interests, and response to setbacks, individuals can gain insights into their grit levels.

Beyond formal assessments, self-reflection is crucial. Consider your past pursuits and accomplishments: Have you demonstrated sustained effort and passion toward long-term goals? How have you responded to failures and obstacles? Reflecting on these experiences can help identify areas where you exhibit grit and areas that may need further development.

Developing grit involves cultivating a growth mindset, as proposed by Carol Dweck. Embrace challenges, view failures as opportunities to learn, and maintain a long-term perspective on your goals. Surround yourself with supportive individuals who encourage perseverance and provide constructive feedback. Engaging in activities challenging and pushing you out of your comfort zone can also help build grit.

Practicing mindfulness and stress management techniques can further support the development of grit. These practices help individuals maintain emotional regulation and focus, which are critical for persevering through difficult times. Setting realistic, incremental goals and celebrating small achievements along the way can also reinforce a gritty mindset.

Understanding grit involves recognizing its historical significance, exploring the psychological and physiological mechanisms behind it, learning from famous examples, and assessing one's own level of grit. By cultivating this powerful trait, individuals can enhance their ability to achieve long-term goals and overcome challenges, ultimately leading to greater personal and professional fulfillment. Grit is not just an innate quality but a skill that can be developed and strengthened through deliberate practice and a commitment to one's passions and goals.

5 STEP ACTION PLAN

Assess Your Grit	**Take Notice of Your Grit**: Measure your level of grit by knowing what drives you. How much time are you dedicating to these items? What are you ignoring or what are facing that requires you to focus on completing. **Reflect on Past Experiences**: Consider how you've handled long-term goals and setbacks. The setbacks require your own grit to complete.
Cultivate a Growth Mindset	**Embrace Challenges**: View obstacles as opportunities for growth. **Practice Positive Self-Talk**: Focus on progress and resilience, not setbacks.
Set Clear, Long-Term Goals	**Align Goals with Your Passion**: Ensure your goals resonate deeply with you. **Break Down Goals**: Divide long-term objectives into smaller, achievable steps.
Stay Physically and Mentally Fit	**Maintain a Healthy Lifestyle**: Proper sleep, nutrition, and exercise support brain function and resilience. **Engage in Brain-Boosting Activities**: Foster neuroplasticity with challenging mental exercises.
Celebrate Progress and Reflect	**Acknowledge Small Wins**: Celebrate milestones to stay motivated. **Reflect Regularly**: Assess what works and refine your approach.

2

The Role of Gratitude

DEFINITION AND CULTURAL SIGNIFICANCE

Gratitude is the quality of being thankful and the readiness to show appreciation for and to return kindness. This simple yet profound concept has roots in various cultures and traditions around the world, playing a significant role in human interaction and social bonding. In many ancient civilizations, gratitude was not merely an emotion but a critical component of societal well-being.

In Eastern philosophies, such as Buddhism and Confucianism, gratitude is seen as a vital virtue. It encourages people to acknowledge the interconnectedness of all beings and to appreciate the roles that others play in their lives. In the Western world, gratitude has been emphasized through religious and philosophical teachings. For instance, the Bible and other religious texts underscore the importance of thankfulness as a moral duty and spiritual practice.

Across different cultures, gratitude rituals and traditions vary but share a common thread: recognizing and honoring the contributions and support of others. Whether it's through a simple thank-you note, a public acknowledgment, or more elaborate ceremonies, gratitude serves as a bridge that connects individuals, strengthens relationships, and fosters a sense of community.

As a part of understanding gratitude, it is also key to be knowledgeable about what is the opposite or contrast to it. The most direct opposite of gratitude is ingratitude which is lack of appreciation, thankfulness, or acknowledgement. Other forms of contrast is entitlement, resentment, envy, complaining, and apathy.

A STORY OF DR. JEFF DOCKING

As someone I've had the pleasure of partnering with over the years, I've witnessed firsthand President Docking's deep care and unwavering dedication to his students. He is a leader with both the grit to accomplish his goals and the humility to pause and listen to the voices of his students at Adrian College, as well as those who help shape his perspective. That's why I knew I had to reach out to him for this book. Here's the reason.

Docking grew up in Michigan, spending part of his childhood, starting in the second grade, living in the Michigan State University dormitories while his father pursued a doctorate. During this period, he became a fan of the Michigan State Spartans men's ice hockey team and worked as a stick boy. After his father completed his studies, he became the deputy superintendent of East Lansing Public Schools.

After earning his undergraduate degree from Michigan State University, Docking briefly worked as a reporter for WFSL-TV in Lansing, covering the Michigan State Capitol. He later left the job to attend Garrett-Evangelical Theological Seminary, where he earned a Master of Divinity (M.Div.) degree. He then pursued a Ph.D. in social ethics at Boston University, supporting himself by working as a residence hall director in the university's dormitories.

This passage highlights a deep sense of grit, emphasizing the importance of knowing both what needs to be accomplished and the time it will take. During our conversation, I asked Docking where his grit originates, and he shared that he is a builder and creator, someone who approaches every day as if it starts from zero. This starting-from-zero mentality is a common trait among those with significant grit who view the world as something they are destined to conquer. They have unwavering confidence in their abilities and fulfill their purpose through their daily work. There's a competitive spirit in them, often unnoticed by others, as they quietly strive for greatness.

Docking explained that simply showing up is one component of grit, but it's perseverance that truly distinguishes the ordinary from the extraordinary—or, as I like to say, the uncommon from the uncommon. What stood out most was how Docking's grit and gratitude were instilled early in his life, inspired by Martin Luther King Jr. and his studies on building a nonviolent society. Docking has since embodied a work ethic where no one can outwork him in his role as President of Adrian College. And I agree – he has my vote of confidence, every day.

In a recent podcast, Docking delved deeper into his daily commitment to cultivating grit. He emphasized the importance of consistency, noting that simply showing up—day in and day out—is a critical factor in achieving long-term success. Docking pointed out that opportunities often arise when people pursue goals that not only benefit themselves but also create value for others, leading to mutually beneficial outcomes. He also discussed the power of building a strong network, explaining how it can amplify both reach and resilience, particularly when that network is aligned with a clear mission and purpose. This perspective aligns with his belief that individuals with a high level of grit often possess an entrepreneurial mindset, marked by perseverance, adaptability, and a willingness to take calculated risks in pursuit of their goals.

In reflecting on President Docking's journey and his deeply ingrained sense of grit, it becomes clear why he stands out as a leader who not only talks the talk but walks the walk. His ability to build meaningful relationships, coupled with his unwavering work ethic, demonstrates a leadership style rooted in both perseverance and purpose. Through his life's work—whether as a student, a spiritual scholar, or as the president of Adrian College—Docking has consistently embraced the mindset of starting from zero, creating value for others, and leading by example. His daily commitment to showing up and persevering, even in the face of challenges, is what truly sets him apart. It's no wonder that his students, faculty, and colleagues have such deep respect for him, and why I felt compelled to include his story in this book. His is a story not just of grit but of gratitude, service, and an unwavering pursuit of excellence.

THE SCIENCE OF GRATITUDE: UNRAVELING THE PSYCHOLOGICAL AND PHYSIOLOGICAL BENEFITS

Imagine a simple habit that could reshape your mind, recalibrate your emotions, and even alter the way your body functions. That habit is gratitude—a practice that, for centuries, has been woven into spiritual and philosophical teachings but is only now being understood through the lens of modern science. New research in psychology and neuroscience is peeling back the layers, showing that gratitude does far more than just make us feel good. It has the potential to rewire our brains, buffer us from stress, and strengthen our physical health in remarkable ways.

A WINDOW INTO THE MIND AND BODY

Gratitude, often perceived as a fleeting emotion, is far more than just a brief sense of appreciation. It is a state of being that has long-lasting effects on how we perceive the world, how we relate to others, and even how our brains are structured. Let's journey through the science to explore how the simple act of giving thanks can alter your mental and physical health.

ENHANCED MENTAL HEALTH: REFRAMING STRESS AND DEPRESSION

Gratitude acts as a powerful antidote to mental distress. Picture this: when life's pressures begin to mount, our minds naturally drift toward negativity—an evolutionary trait meant to keep us alert to dangers. But chronic negativity erodes mental health. Gratitude intervenes here by shifting focus to what is positive and meaningful in life. Studies show that individuals who practice gratitude regularly experience significantly lower levels of depression and anxiety. This isn't magic; it's neuroscience. Gratitude activates brain regions associated with the regulation of emotions, particularly the prefrontal cortex, creating an emotional buffer that helps reduce stress and promotes a more balanced mood. By reframing our thoughts, gratitude allows us to see challenges not as insurmountable but as manageable, thereby reducing the mental weight we carry.

IMPROVED RELATIONSHIPS: THE CYCLE OF APPRECIATION

Human connection thrives on reciprocity, and gratitude acts as a social glue. Imagine the ripple effect of a simple "thank you." When expressed sincerely, gratitude triggers a response in the receiver—a sense of being valued and appreciated. This, in turn, encourages them to reciprocate those feelings, fostering a positive feedback loop in relationships. Over time, this exchange deepens trust, strengthens bonds, and enhances social connections. This effect is not limited to personal relationships; workplaces that cultivate gratitude see improvements in team cohesion, collaboration, and overall morale. When people feel valued, they are more likely to go the extra mile—not out of obligation but out of genuine connection.

INCREASED RESILIENCE: GRATITUDE AS AN EMOTIONAL SHIELD

Resilience, the ability to bounce back from adversity, is a trait often admired but difficult to cultivate. Gratitude plays a pivotal role here. Grateful individuals are more likely to view setbacks as temporary rather than catastrophic. Why? Because gratitude fosters a sense of perspective. It reminds us of the good things we have, even in tough times. This shift in focus boosts self-worth and strengthens emotional endurance, allowing individuals to navigate life's inevitable challenges with greater ease. Gratitude acts like an emotional shock absorber, softening the impact of negative events and reducing the likelihood of feeling overwhelmed.

BRAIN STRUCTURE CHANGES: GRATITUDE REWIRES THE BRAIN

The brain is an incredibly adaptable organ, constantly reshaping itself based on our experiences—a phenomenon known as neuroplasticity. Gratitude, it turns out, can be a catalyst for this reshaping. Functional MRI scans reveal that regular gratitude practices increase activity in the prefrontal cortex, the area of the brain responsible for planning, decision-making, and emotional regulation. These changes suggest that practicing gratitude doesn't just make us feel good in the moment—it strengthens our ability to manage emotions long-term. Over time, the brain becomes more adept at recognizing and focusing on positive stimuli, leading to an overall improvement in emotional well-being.

DOPAMINE: THE BRAIN'S REWARD SYSTEM ON OVERDRIVE

Dopamine, often called the "feel-good" neurotransmitter, is central to how we experience pleasure and motivation. Gratitude, by stimulating the hypothalamus—a region of the brain involved in regulating stress and emotions—triggers the release of dopamine. This surge in dopamine levels boosts mood, enhances life satisfaction, and creates a positive feedback loop that encourages us to continue practicing gratitude. The more we express gratitude, the more our brain's reward circuits are activated, making it easier to cultivate a positive outlook.

BETTER SLEEP: RESTORATIVE BENEFITS OF A GRATEFUL MIND

Sleep is a critical component of health, yet many struggle with insomnia or poor-quality rest. Gratitude, it seems, can offer a natural remedy. Research has shown that individuals who regularly engage in gratitude practices, such as keeping a gratitude journal, tend to fall asleep faster and enjoy better sleep quality. The mechanism is simple: gratitude promotes positive thoughts while dampening anxiety and intrusive thoughts that often keep people awake. By focusing on what we are grateful for, we reduce the mental clutter that can disrupt sleep, allowing for a more peaceful transition into rest.

REDUCED PHYSICAL SYMPTOMS: THE BODY RESPONDS TO GRATITUDE

The mind and body are deeply interconnected, and gratitude has been shown to reduce the physical manifestations of stress. Studies have found that individuals who regularly practice gratitude report fewer physical symptoms such as headaches, muscle tension, and even chronic pain. This could be due to gratitude's ability to lower cortisol levels, the body's primary stress hormone. Lower cortisol levels mean reduced inflammation and better immune function, both of which contribute to fewer physical ailments. Gratitude, in this sense, acts as a buffer against the wear and tear that chronic stress can inflict on the body.

IMPROVED HEART HEALTH: THE HEARTFELT IMPACT OF GRATITUDE

Gratitude's benefits extend all the way to the heart—literally. Grateful individuals tend to have lower blood pressure, better heart rate variability (a marker of cardiovascular health), and overall improved cardiac function. The link between gratitude and heart health is likely tied to stress reduction. Chronic stress is a known contributor to heart disease, but by fostering positive emotions and reducing stress hormones, gratitude helps protect the heart from these harmful effects. In this way, gratitude not only strengthens emotional well-being but also supports one of the most vital organs in the body.

THE GRATITUDE PRACTICE AS A LIFE-ALTERING TOOL

Gratitude is more than just a feel-good emotion. It is a powerful tool that reshapes both the mind and body, enhancing mental health, fostering deeper relationships, increasing resilience, and even improving physical health. In a world that often focuses on what's lacking, gratitude offers a way to center on what's abundant, shifting our perspective from scarcity to sufficiency. Whether through daily journaling, meditative reflection, or simply making a habit of saying "thank you," the practice of gratitude holds the potential to transform your life from the inside out.

STORIES OF GRATITUDE FROM DIVERSE BACKGROUNDS

Gratitude transcends cultural and geographical boundaries, manifesting in unique ways across the globe. Here are a few stories that highlight the universal power of gratitude:

A Vietnamese Tradition

In Vietnamese culture, a similar practice that reflects deep appreciation and respect is seen in the tradition of "Tất niên," the Lunar New Year's Eve celebration. This practice involves the "cúng ông Công ông Táo» ritual, where families give thanks to the Kitchen Gods (Táo Quân) and the household›s ancestors. The Kitchen Gods are believed to report on the family›s affairs to the Jade Emperor in Heaven.

During this ritual, the family prepares offerings, including food, incense, and paper effigies, which are burned to send the gods back to heaven. The offerings are presented with deep gratitude for the protection and blessings the Kitchen Gods and ancestors have provided throughout the year.

This practice, like the Asian tea ceremony, emphasizes mindfulness and respect for the elements that contribute to the well-being of the household. By expressing gratitude to the gods and ancestors, the family acknowledges the interconnectedness of life and honors the spiritual forces that are believed to influence their lives. This tradition teaches the importance of appreciation, reverence, and recognition of the unseen forces that play a role in daily life.

An African Village

In many African cultures, gratitude is expressed communally. In one village, it is customary for the entire community to come together to celebrate a successful harvest. They hold a festival where they thank the land, the weather, and each other for their collective effort. This practice reinforces community bonds and instills a deep appreciation for nature and mutual support.

During the festival, villagers participate in traditional dances, songs, and rituals that honor the earth and the ancestors who are believed to have blessed the harvest. They share stories of their challenges during the planting season and express gratitude for the communal efforts that led to their success. This collective expression of gratitude strengthens social cohesion and reminds everyone of the importance of working together and supporting one another.

A WESTERN WORKPLACE

In a Western corporate setting, a manager implemented a gratitude practice by starting meetings with a round of thank-yous. Employees would take turns expressing gratitude for their colleagues' contributions. This simple practice transformed the workplace culture, fostering a more positive, collaborative, and motivated team environment.

For example, during one meeting, an employee thanked a colleague for staying late to help finish a project, which led to its timely completion. This public acknowledgment not only boosted the morale of the appreciated employee but also inspired others to express their gratitude. Over time, this practice created a culture of recognition and appreciation, where employees felt valued and motivated to support each other. The ripple effect of gratitude improved overall job satisfaction and productivity.

AN INDIGENOUS RITUAL

In the Iroquois nations, gratitude is integral to daily Haudenosaunee life. Among the Mohawk, Oneida, Onondaga, Cayuga, Seneca, and Tuscarora tribes, for instance, the "Words That Come Before All Else" is recited to give thanks to all elements of the natural world. This practice instills a deep sense of interconnectedness and responsibility toward the environment and each other.

The "Words That Come Before All Else" is often recited at the beginning of gatherings and ceremonies. It acknowledges and thanks the earth, the waters, the plants, the animals, the winds, and the celestial bodies for their contributions to life. These rituals express gratitude and reinforce the community's commitment to protecting and honoring the natural world. Regularly reciting the Thanksgiving Address reminds individuals of their place within the larger ecosystem and their duty to care for it.

A REFUGEE'S GRATITUDE

After resettling in a new country, a Syrian refugee expressed profound gratitude to the local community that welcomed and supported him. He started volunteering at a community center, offering language lessons and cultural exchange sessions. His gratitude helped him integrate and enrich the lives of those he helped.

This refugee's journey began with immense challenges, but the support and kindness he received from his new neighbors inspired him to give back. By teaching language classes, he helped other newcomers navigate their new environment more quickly. His cultural exchange sessions allowed locals to learn about Syrian culture, fostering mutual understanding and appreciation. His story highlights how gratitude can inspire acts of kindness and create bridges between diverse communities.

A Story Of Angela Cheng-Cimini

Angela Cheng-Cimini, a distinguished Asian leader, exemplifies a remarkable blend of grit and gratitude, traits that are evident not only in her professional achievements but also in her grounded presence. I, Adam, had the privilege of meeting Angela over the past year and have since followed her journey through LinkedIn and various other professional venues where we both have had the opportunity to speak. It is my firm belief that the foundations of grit and gratitude are laid in the early stages of one's life, and after engaging deeply with Angela, I am compelled to share her story.

Angela's formative years were significantly shaped by her parents, whose guidance continues to influence her approach to leadership and life. A phrase she frequently uses, "Pay it forward, to pay it back," captures a core value ingrained in her from a young age.

This maxim speaks to a philosophy of reciprocity and generosity, values deeply embedded in her Eastern upbringing. Navigating her path from an Eastern cultural background to achieving professional excellence within the context of Western corporate culture is an endeavor fraught with challenges—challenges that Angela has navigated with a unique combination of grit and gratitude.

What is particularly commendable about Angela is her ability to remain humble while driving impactful change in her work. Her career began at

Citibank, where she focused on analytics related to Diversity, Equity, Inclusion, and Belonging (DEIB). It is here that Angela seems to have discovered and leaned into her deeper purpose: to amplify the voices of those who may not speak out, to share stories with authenticity rather than boastfulness, and to empower others to craft their personal narratives while sustaining the energy to "pay it forward." Her approach is not about self-promotion but rather about uplifting others and fostering a culture of inclusion and belonging.

Angela also shared a profound insight into the nature of grit—the "multiplier effect" that occurs when one is surrounded by others who share the same objectives and values. This idea is pivotal not only for recharging one's sense of determination but also for mitigating the risk of burnout. During our conversation, Angela emphasized the importance of alignment among one's body, brain, and heart—a principle that she considers vital for sustained success. When I asked her about the most impactful advice she has either received or would impart, she articulated, "If your body, brain, and heart are not aligned, something is not working."

This advice speaks to the nuanced understanding that grit is not merely about pushing through adversity; it is also about recognizing when you are out of sync with your true purpose.

When we find ourselves working against the grain, the dissonance becomes apparent—not only in our thoughts but in our overall sense of well-being. Days may feel unfulfilled, self-doubt may creep in more often, and relationships may become strained because the energy we are expending does not yield our best selves. Angela's wisdom encourages us to trust our grit when our work feels natural and aligned, suggesting that when the effort feels fluid and intuitive, we are likely on the right path forward.

Angela Cheng-Cimini's journey is a testament to the power of combining grit with gratitude, of leading with humility while being firmly grounded in one's purpose. Her story serves as a powerful reminder that true leadership involves not just the courage to persevere but also the wisdom to align one's inner and outer worlds in pursuit of meaningful impact.

MEASURING YOUR GRATITUDE: A DEEPER DIVE INTO TRANSFORMING YOUR PERSPECTIVE

Gratitude is more than a fleeting feeling—it's a mindset, a way of navigating the world with appreciation for what we have, who we are, and how we connect with others. But how do we measure something as intangible as gratitude? In this chapter, we'll explore methods that not only help you assess your gratitude levels but also cultivate a deeper, more consistent practice. By doing so, you can harness the profound benefits of gratitude, from emotional well-being to resilience in the face of adversity.

THE POWER OF A GRATITUDE JOURNAL: SHIFTING FOCUS, TRANSFORMING MINDSET

Imagine waking up each morning with a mind racing toward the tasks, challenges, or worries that lie ahead. Now, contrast that with the simple act of taking a pen, opening a journal, and noting three things you're genuinely grateful for. The beauty of a gratitude journal lies in its ability to reframe your mindset. This daily ritual, though seemingly small, trains your brain to shift focus away from what's missing to what is already present.

Consider writing down a moment of kindness from a stranger or the warmth of sunlight filtering through your window as you sip your morning coffee. Over time, this practice rewires the brain to notice and appreciate the small but significant moments that make life rich. It turns mundane aspects of your day into reminders of abundance, helping you see challenges in the context of blessings.

But the true power of this practice is revealed over time. When you reflect back on past entries, you relive those moments of gratitude, reinforcing their emotional impact. That kind gesture from a colleague, or the quiet joy of a Sunday morning walk, now serves as an emotional anchor, reminding you of the positivity woven into your life, even during difficult times.

Quantifying Gratitude: The Science Behind Surveys

While gratitude journals tap into personal reflection, how can we objectively measure gratitude? Enter tools like the **Gratitude Questionnaire (GQ-6)**, a scientific method designed to gauge gratitude levels. This tool asks you to rate your agreement with statements like, "I have so much in life to be thankful for" or "I am grateful to a wide variety of people."

What makes this method powerful is its ability to reveal patterns and blind spots in your gratitude practice. For example, perhaps you're consistently thankful for your achievements, but the questionnaire highlights an area where you can focus more—like gratitude for people in your life. It also provides a benchmark, so you can measure your growth as you incorporate more gratitude practices.

Think of the GQ-6 as a mirror, reflecting back the nuances of your emotional landscape. By revisiting it periodically, you track not only how your gratitude grows but also how life's challenges shape and deepen your appreciation for the world around you.

Reflective Practices: Cultivating Awareness of the Good

Reflection is a quiet yet profound act. Imagine ending your day with a brief mental review of what went well and who contributed to those moments. This doesn't have to be a formal meditation or a written practice, but can simply be a few minutes of mindful reflection.

Each day, life offers an abundance of moments that can easily go unnoticed: a smile exchanged in passing, a supportive word from a friend, or the satisfaction of completing a project. By actively reflecting on these moments, you create a habit of noticing and acknowledging the good.

This practice not only shifts your focus to what went well, but it also builds a narrative of interconnectedness—recognizing how often others contribute to your well-being. The outcome is a quieter, more grounded sense of gratitude, anchored in the subtle and fleeting experiences that make life meaningful.

Acts of Kindness: Gratitude in Action

True gratitude isn't confined to thoughts and feelings—it's expressed in action. Engaging in acts of kindness allows you to give back to others while simultaneously reinforcing your own gratitude. Each act, no matter how small, has the potential to create a ripple effect of positivity.

Think about it: offering a helping hand to a colleague, mentoring a younger professional, or volunteering at a local organization not only lifts others up, but it also heightens your awareness of your own blessings. It connects you to something larger than yourself, fostering a sense of purpose and belonging.

Research shows that when we actively help others, our brain's reward systems are activated. This isn't just about feeling good—it's about recognizing how giving to others enhances your own emotional well-being. Kindness, in this sense, becomes a two-way street: benefiting both the giver and the receiver, all while deepening your gratitude for the opportunity to contribute.

Gratitude Letters and Visits: Strengthening Relationships Through Expression

There are few experiences as powerful as writing a heartfelt letter to someone who has profoundly impacted your life. A gratitude letter, when delivered in person, becomes a transformative experience for both you and the recipient.

Take a moment to think of someone who has made a lasting difference in your life—a mentor, a teacher, or a friend. Writing to them not only forces you to articulate your gratitude in a concrete way, but it also strengthens your emotional connection to that person. Reading the letter aloud amplifies the experience, making the gratitude real, tangible, and shared. The exchange often leads to an emotional and lasting bond, one that deepens your sense of connection and appreciation for the people in your life.

EMBRACING DIGITAL GRATITUDE PRACTICES: TECHNOLOGY AS A TOOL FOR CONNECTION

In a world where our phones are never far from reach, why not leverage technology to support your gratitude practice? Apps like **Happify** and **Gratitude** offer structured activities, journaling prompts, and reminders that help you integrate gratitude into your daily life.

These platforms also connect you to a larger community of gratitude practitioners, creating a virtual space where you can share experiences, find inspiration, and reinforce your practice. The digital world can become a supportive ecosystem, fostering an ongoing dialogue of gratitude that extends beyond your immediate circle and deepens your connection to others.

CULTIVATING A GRATITUDE MINDSET: A LIFELONG JOURNEY

Gratitude is not a destination; it's a journey that requires consistent practice, mindfulness, and a willingness to see beyond the obvious. Developing this mindset means intentionally training your brain to notice the good amidst life's challenges.

Consider practicing mindful awareness, where you focus on the present moment and find joy in the small, everyday experiences that often go unnoticed. Or reframe challenges as opportunities for growth, recognizing the strength and resilience gained through adversity. Surround yourself with people who value gratitude, and actively engage in communities that promote positive thinking. Finally, create daily rituals that center gratitude—whether it's a morning reflection or an evening gratitude walk.

By intentionally cultivating gratitude, you transform your life from one of scarcity and longing to one of abundance and fulfillment. Gratitude becomes not just a fleeting feeling, but a core part of who you are, shaping your perspective, your relationships, and ultimately, your sense of purpose in the world.

Gratitude is a powerful force that can transform individuals and communities. By understanding its significance, recognizing its benefits, and actively practicing it, we can create a more connected, resilient, and joyful world. As we continue to explore the role of gratitude in our lives, we discover that it is not just an emotion but a way of being that enriches our existence and enhances our collective well-being.

EXPLORE GRATITUDE IN DIVINE AND NATURAL PRATICES AND BELIEFS

Gratitude, a universal principle deeply embedded in numerous faith traditions, plays a significant role in fostering a harmonious relationship with the divine or the natural world. It is a common theme in many religious beliefs and practices worldwide, from expressing thanks to a higher power to acknowledging life's interconnectedness and appreciating the blessings and challenges that shape human existence. Gratitude fosters a sense of humility, compassion, and interconnectedness, encouraging individuals to recognize and appreciate the positive aspects of their lives and the contributions of others. Religions often aim to cultivate inner peace and community cohesion by promoting a mindset of thankfulness.

Gratitude, a universal theme in many religious beliefs and practices worldwide, serves as a unifying force that connects individuals across different faith traditions.

1. Christianity: Gratitude is a central theme, often expressed in prayers, hymns, and liturgy. The Bible frequently encourages believers to give thanks to God. For example, 1 Thessalonians 5:18 says, "Give thanks in all circumstances; for this is God's will for you in Christ Jesus."

2. Islam: Gratitude (shukr) is emphasized in the Quran and Hadith. Muslims are encouraged to be grateful to Allah for all blessings and to express this gratitude through prayers and good deeds. The Quran states, "If you are grateful, I will surely increase you [in favor]" (Quran 14:7).

3. Judaism: Gratitude is a significant aspect of Jewish worship and daily life. Prayers of thanks are a regular part of Jewish rituals, such as the Shema and the Amidah. The Hebrew Bible (Tanakh) also contains many passages emphasizing the importance of thanking God.

4. Buddhism: While not centered on a deity, Buddhism teaches gratitude as a powerful tool to develop positive mental states and reduce suffering. Practitioners are encouraged to express gratitude for their teachers, the Dharma (teachings), and the Sangha (community). This emphasis on gratitude offers a beacon of hope, reminding us that even in the face of suffering, there is always something to be thankful for.

5. Hinduism: Gratitude is expressed through various rituals and practices, including offerings and prayers to deities. Hindus often thank the divine for blessings and guidance in their lives.

6. Sikhism: Gratitude is crucial to Sikh practice. Sikhs thank their god through daily prayers, meditation, and community service. The Guru Granth Sahib, the holy scripture of Sikhism, contains many hymns of gratitude.

Gratitude in religious contexts strengthens the relationship between the practitioner and the divine or the spiritual aspects of life, fostering a sense of humility and interconnectedness. Exploring gratitude through divine and natural beliefs and practices can offer profound insights into its significance for personal well-being and communal harmony. Seek to understand gratitude in these faith-based contexts:

1. Cultural Perspective: It provides a lens into diverse cultural attitudes towards thankfulness, revealing how societies cultivate and express gratitude through rituals and beliefs.

2. Gratitude, as a catalyst for spiritual growth, inspires individuals to reflect on the blessings in their lives, fostering a deeper appreciation for the interconnectedness of all beings and the natural world.

3. Ethical Framework: It offers an ethical framework for living, emphasizing virtues such as humility, compassion, and generosity that are often intertwined with expressions of gratitude.

4. Community Building: It strengthens communal bonds by encouraging gratitude towards others and fostering empathy and belonging within religious or spiritual communities.

Overall, exploring gratitude through divine and natural beliefs and practices enriches one's understanding.

5 STEP ACTION GUIDE

Understand the Meaning and Significance of Gratitude	**Reflect on the Definition**: Spend time understanding the true meaning of gratitude. It's more than just saying "thank you"; it involves a deep appreciation for the interconnectedness of all beings and the contributions of others in your life. **Learn from Cultural Practices**: Study how different cultures, such as those in Japan, Africa, and among Indigenous communities, incorporate gratitude into their daily lives. This understanding will help you appreciate the universal power of gratitude and inspire you to integrate similar practices.
Start a Daily Gratitude Practice	**Gratitude Journaling**: Dedicate a few minutes each day to write down three things you are grateful for. This could be simple moments, like a kind gesture from a friend or a beautiful sunset. Over time, this practice will help shift your focus from what you lack to what you have. **Reflective Practices**: Spend a few moments daily reflecting on positive experiences and who contributed to those moments. This can be done silently, through meditation, or by sharing thoughts with a loved one. **Gratitude Rituals**: Incorporate small rituals, such as a morning gratitude reflection or a bedtime gratitude list, to help you focus on positive aspects of your life consistently.

Engage in Acts of Kindness	**Volunteer and Help Others**: Acts of kindness, such as volunteering, mentoring, or helping a neighbor, are ways to express gratitude. These actions create a ripple effect of positivity and foster a sense of community. **Participate in Communal Gratitude Events**: Engage in communal activities that express gratitude, such as local community events or cultural festivals. These activities help reinforce community bonds and promote collective gratitude.
Reframe Challenges as Opportunities for Growth	**Adopt a Positive Mindset**: When facing setbacks, focus on the lessons learned and the strengths gained from difficult experiences. This approach will help you develop a more resilient and grateful mindset. **Practice Mindful Awareness**: Engage in mindfulness meditation to enhance your ability to notice and appreciate the positive aspects of your day. This practice helps you stay present and cultivate gratitude for even the smallest joys in life.
Incorporate Gratitude in the Workplace	**Implement Gratitude Practices at Work**: If you are in a leadership role or part of a team, suggest starting meetings with a round of thank-yous. Encouraging employees to express gratitude for their colleagues' contributions can transform the workplace culture, fostering positivity, collaboration, and motivation.

Cultivating Grit

Grit is not merely a fleeting burst of motivation or a surge of adrenaline; it is the quiet, unyielding force that propels individuals forward even when the odds seem insurmountable. It's the difference between the person who gives up after the first failure and the one who uses that failure as a stepping stone toward eventual success. To understand grit, we must look beyond the surface and into its core—what really makes a person able to persist when others falter?

At its essence, grit is the relentless pursuit of goals, but more than that, it is the capacity to endure discomfort, uncertainty, and setbacks without losing sight of the bigger picture. Grit asks something of us that's counterintuitive to our nature—when we encounter obstacles, we're wired to retreat, to conserve energy. But grit demands the opposite. It requires us to push forward when every fiber of our being screams to stop.

Consider this: the path to any significant achievement is rarely a straight line. It's littered with obstacles, failures, and moments of doubt. Picture a mountain climber struggling against the icy wind, unsure of the next step but pressing forward, one painstaking foot in front of the other, despite the growing fatigue. That's what grit feels like—not glamorous, but powerful in its persistence.

In this chapter, we delve into the components that make grit so essential for success.

DEVELOPING A GROWTH MINDSET

The concept of developing a growth mindset, as emphasized by Dr. Andrew Huberman, has powerful applications in both personal and professional development.

WORKPLACE DEVELOPMENT

In the workplace, adopting a growth mindset fosters a culture of continuous learning, innovation, and adaptability. Employees who believe they can improve their skills are more likely to take on challenges, learn from feedback, and persist in the face of setbacks. This mindset is critical in fast-paced industries where innovation and learning are essential for staying competitive.

A growth mindset also promotes **resilience in leadership**. Leaders who model and encourage this mindset inspire their teams to approach problems with a positive attitude, embrace new responsibilities, and remain motivated during adversity. Leaders can cultivate a more collaborative and open work environment by focusing on learning and improvement rather than being defensive about mistakes.

EMPLOYEE ENGAGEMENT AND MOTIVATION

Employees with a growth mindset feel more engaged because they see their work as an opportunity to grow and develop, rather than just fulfilling static expectations. They are more likely to seek out challenges, contribute new ideas, and pursue continuous improvement. This mindset reduces fear of failure and increases job satisfaction and retention.

Encouraging a growth mindset among employees can directly counteract **workplace isolation and loneliness.** When people view struggles as opportunities to develop, they are more likely to collaborate, share ideas, and seek mentorship. This creates a culture of support and engagement, reducing feelings of isolation.

EMOTIONAL RESILIENCE AND STRESS MANAGEMENT

A growth mindset also contributes to emotional resilience. Viewing setbacks as learning opportunities helps individuals cope with stress and pressure, reducing the likelihood of burnout. This can be particularly important in high-stress jobs, where a fixed mindset might lead to frustration, disengagement, and low morale.

Resilience also strengthens one's ability to manage relationships, both professionally and personally. In the workplace, growth-minded individuals are more likely to give and receive feedback constructively, improve their interpersonal skills, and maintain positive, productive relationships even in difficult circumstances.

INNOVATION AND PROBLEM-SOLVING

A growth mindset encourages creativity and risk-taking. When individuals or teams believe that effort and learning lead to improvement, they are more willing to explore unconventional solutions and challenge existing methods. This leads to greater innovation and more effective problem-solving.

CONNECTION TO GRIT

As Huberman points out, grit is built upon a growth mindset, which is defined as passion and perseverance toward long-term goals. The belief that you can improve through effort helps sustain perseverance. This directly links to success, as people with grit tend to achieve more over the long term, not because they never fail but because they continue to learn and grow through failure.

The growth mindset is a fundamental driver for personal development, leadership, and team success. It creates environments where learning, innovation, and resilience thrive, contributing to individual and organizational growth.

EMBRACING CHALLENGES AS LEARNING OPPORTUNITIES

A growth mindset transforms the perception of challenges. Instead of viewing difficult tasks as threats, see them as opportunities to expand your skills and knowledge. This shift in perspective encourages continuous learning and resilience.

For instance, if you encounter a complex project at work, approach it as a chance to develop new competencies rather than feeling overwhelmed. Seek out resources, ask for help, and break the project into smaller, manageable tasks. Each step you take enhances your abilities and boosts your confidence.

CELEBRATING EFFORT AND PROGRESS

A key aspect of a growth mindset is valuing effort over innate talent. Celebrate your hard work and progress, regardless of the outcome. Focusing on effort helps you stay motivated and fosters a positive attitude toward learning and improvement.

Consider maintaining a journal where you document your efforts, milestones, and the lessons you learn. Reflecting on your journey can provide valuable insights and reinforce your commitment to growth.

PRACTICAL STEPS TO FOSTER A GROWTH MINDSET

ENCOURAGING CONTINUOUS LEARNING AND DEVELOPMENT

One of the most effective ways to embed a growth mindset in the workplace is by promoting continuous learning. This can be done by:

- **Providing Learning Opportunities:** Offer employees access to online courses, workshops, or mentorship programs to develop their skills. Encourage cross-training between departments to expose employees to different functions and challenges.
- **Emphasizing Learning Over Perfection:** In meetings or performance reviews, focus on what employees have learned from projects, especially when things didn't go as planned. Shifting the focus from perfect outcomes to learning experiences signals that growth is valued.
- **Recognizing Effort and Growth:** Praise employees not only for their success but also for their effort and persistence. This reinforces the idea that growth comes from hard work and perseverance rather than innate talent alone.

Example: In a marketing department, rather than focusing solely on campaign success metrics, a manager could celebrate the creative process, the testing of new strategies, and what the team learned from both successful and less successful initiatives.

CREATING A CULTURE OF CONSTRUCTIVE FEEDBACK

Feedback is a powerful tool to cultivate a growth mindset in teams. Constructive feedback encourages improvement and helps employees see challenges as opportunities to grow.

- **Normalize Feedback:** Make feedback a regular part of the work culture. Not just top-down feedback from managers, but peer-to-peer feedback and self-reflection.
- **Promote a Growth-Oriented Approach:** When providing feedback, focus on areas of growth rather than labeling performance as "good" or "bad." Highlight ways the employee can improve and offer resources to support their development.
- **Celebrate Small Wins:** Recognize incremental improvements to show that growth is gradual and continuous. This helps maintain motivation and focus on progress.

Example: In project debriefs, a software development team could discuss not only the technical results of their sprint but also the personal growth and team dynamics during the process. Encouraging reflections on individual and collective growth fosters a sense of progress.

Encouraging Collaboration and Knowledge Sharing

Loneliness and isolation can be significant issues in the workplace, especially in remote or hybrid environments. To address this, implement strategies that build connection and learning among colleagues.

- **Promote Team Learning:** Create platforms where employees can share knowledge, lessons learned, and strategies with each other. This could take the form of regular knowledge-sharing meetings, intranet forums, or even informal "lunch and learn" sessions.
- **Team-Based Problem Solving:** Assign collaborative projects that encourage people to solve problems together. This fosters a sense of shared purpose, helping employees build strong bonds through cooperation.
- **Mentorship Programs:** Implement a mentorship system where senior employees coach newer team members. This not only builds a learning culture but also creates more meaningful connections between colleagues.

Example: A customer support team could hold bi-weekly problem-solving sessions where agents share difficult cases they encountered and how they handled them. More experienced agents could offer tips, and the entire team could benefit from each other's expertise, helping them grow together.

Modeling a Growth Mindset as a Leader

Leaders play a critical role in setting the tone for a growth-oriented workplace. To foster this mindset, leaders should:

- **Be Transparent About Your Own Learning Journey:** Share stories of your own challenges and how you've grown through them. This helps employees understand that learning is a lifelong process, even for those in leadership roles.

- **Encourage Risk-Taking and Innovation:** Create an environment where employees feel safe to take risks and innovate without fear of judgment. When mistakes happen, use them as learning opportunities rather than occasions for blame.
- **Create a Safe Environment for Vulnerability:** Encourage open communication where employees feel comfortable discussing their struggles and asking for help when needed. This reduces fear and isolation, creating a more connected, supportive team environment.

Example: In a sales department, a leader could share a personal story about a difficult pitch that didn't go well, but highlight how that experience led to key insights that improved future pitches. This demonstrates resilience and continuous learning.

Emphasizing Long-Term Growth and Grit

Encourage employees to take on projects or goals that stretch their abilities and require perseverance over the long term.

- **Set Stretch Goals:** Encourage teams to set challenging, long-term goals that push them beyond their comfort zone. Make sure the goals are meaningful and tied to their career growth.
- **Support Through Challenges:** Provide resources, time, and encouragement to help employees push through difficulties. Recognize the persistence it takes to work on long-term projects, even when success isn't immediately visible.
- **Grit Mentorship:** Pair employees working on long-term, difficult projects with mentors who have overcome similar challenges. This not only provides support but also helps reinforce the importance of resilience and growth.

Example: An engineering team tasked with developing a new product could be given the freedom to experiment with cutting-edge technologies. While the road may be long and full of technical challenges, the company can provide ongoing support, mentorship, and time to foster both personal and professional growth through grit.

IMPLEMENTATION TIPS:

- **Start Small:** Begin by integrating growth mindset conversations into one-on-ones or team meetings. Ask employees what they've learned recently or what challenges they're excited to tackle.
- **Assess Your Culture:** Conduct a survey or open discussion to gauge the current mindset in your organization. Use this feedback to tailor growth mindset initiatives.
- **Reward Growth:** Align rewards and recognition programs with growth-oriented behaviors, like learning new skills, taking risks, and showing resilience.

Implementing these strategies can help foster a workplace culture that values learning, collaboration, and resilience, ultimately improving employee engagement, innovation, and long-term success.

When we talk about goal setting, there's a lot of unnecessary complexity these days. People often overcomplicate the process with acronyms and elaborate steps. But in reality, setting goals should come down to just two things: the 'what' and the 'how.'

The 'what' is the goal itself—what exactly are you trying to achieve? The 'how' is the specific actions or processes that will get you to that goal. A common mistake people make is confusing the two, describing the 'how' as if it's the goal. But remember, the 'what' is the goal, and the 'how' is simply the roadmap to achieving it.

Here are some practical tips for effective goal setting:

SETTING LONG-TERM GOALS AND MAINTAINING FOCUS

Setting long-term goals gives direction and purpose to your efforts. These goals should be ambitious yet achievable, providing a roadmap for your journey. Maintaining focus on these goals requires discipline, planning, and the ability to prioritize.

DEFINING CLEAR OBJECTIVES

Start by defining clear and specific objectives. Vague goals like "I want to be successful" are less effective than precise goals such as "I want to earn a promotion to a managerial position within the next two years." Specificity provides clarity and helps you create a concrete action plan.

BREAKING DOWN GOALS INTO MANAGEABLE TASKS

Long-term goals can seem daunting. Breaking them down into smaller, manageable tasks makes the process less overwhelming and allows you to track progress more easily. Each small step completed is a victory that keeps you motivated.

For example, if your goal is to write a book, break it down into stages: research, outline, chapter drafts, revisions, and final edits. Focus on completing each stage one at a time, eventually leading to accomplishing your larger goal.

CREATING A DETAILED ACTION PLAN

A well-structured action plan outlines the steps needed to achieve your goals. Action plans should include timelines, required resources, and potential obstacles. This plan acts as a roadmap, guiding your efforts and keeping you on track.

STAYING ORGANIZED AND PRIORITIZING

Effective organization and prioritization are crucial for maintaining focus. Use tools like calendars, to-do lists, and project management apps to keep track of your tasks and deadlines. Prioritize activities that directly contribute to your long-term goals, and learn to say no to distractions that do not align with your objectives.

STRATEGIES FOR EFFECTIVE GOAL SETTING AND FOCUS

1. **Define Clear Objectives:** Write down specific, measurable, attainable, relevant, and time-bound (SMART) goals. Know what your aims and outcomes are before starting. Too often, we get tricked by our mindset of saying what the objective is, but it's the outcome. For example, if you say you'll lose weight - that's the outcome. The goal is to eat healthy daily and cut out the junk food.

2. **Break Down Goals:** Divide long-term goals into smaller, manageable tasks. This makes the process less overwhelming and provides regular milestones to celebrate.

3. **Create a Plan:** Develop a detailed action plan outlining the steps needed to achieve your goals. Include timelines and resources required. A key to the plan is consistency on a regular cadence over a period of time.

4. **Stay Organized:** Use tools like calendars, to-do lists, and project management apps to keep track of progress and deadlines.

5. **Limit Distractions:** Identify and minimize sources of distraction. Create a conducive work environment that supports focus and productivity. Limiting distractions is about the self-identification of those tasks that take away your focus. Know what those items are and their limits.

6. **Regularly Review Goals:** Periodically revisit your goals and progress. Adjust your plans as needed to stay on track. A vision board is a terrific and creative way to remind you of the goals regularly.

OVERCOMING OBSTACLES AND SETBACKS

Obstacles and setbacks are inevitable on the path to success. The key to cultivating grit is how you respond to these challenges. Resilience, adaptability, and a positive attitude are crucial in overcoming hurdles.

DEVELOPING RESILIENCE

Resilience is the ability to bounce back from adversity. It involves maintaining a positive outlook, staying flexible, and adapting to new circumstances. Developing resilience starts with accepting that setbacks are a natural part of any journey.

When faced with a setback, take a moment to assess the situation objectively. What went wrong? What can you learn from this experience? Use these insights to adjust your approach and continue moving forward.

MAINTAINING A POSITIVE ATTITUDE

A positive attitude is essential for overcoming obstacles. It helps you stay motivated and focused, even in difficult times. Practice gratitude by regularly reflecting on your life's positive aspects and achievements. This can shift your focus from what is going wrong to what is going right, boosting your overall outlook and resilience.

BUILDING A SUPPORT NETWORK

A strong support network provides encouragement, advice, and a sense of community. Surround yourself with people who believe in your goals and offer constructive feedback. Lean on this network during challenging times to gain new perspectives and stay motivated.

TECHNIQUES FOR OVERCOMING OBSTACLES

1. Stay Positive: Maintain an optimistic outlook, even in adversity. Believe in your ability to overcome challenges.

2. Adapt and Improvise: When faced with obstacles, be flexible and willing to change your approach. Look for alternative solutions and strategies.

3. Seek Support: Surround yourself with a supportive network of friends, family, and mentors. They can provide guidance, encouragement, and fresh perspectives.

4. Learn from Setbacks: Treat failures as learning experiences. Analyze what went wrong, identify lessons learned, and apply them to future efforts.

5. Practice Self-Care: Take care of your physical and mental well-being. Regular exercise, a healthy diet, sufficient sleep, and stress management techniques are essential for resilience.

PRACTICAL EXERCISES AND DAILY HABITS TO BUILD GRIT

Building grit is a multifaceted process deeply rooted in the brain's neuroplasticity—the ability of the brain to change and adapt over time through experience and effort. Grit isn't just about sheer willpower; it's about consistently engaging in behaviors that push the boundaries of your comfort zone and fostering a mindset that embraces challenge.

We would emphasize that the brain's prefrontal cortex, which governs focus, decision-making, and impulse control, plays a crucial role in building grit. This part of the brain helps you override the desire for immediate gratification, allowing you to prioritize long-term goals over short-term comforts. Consistent effort is key here. Through repetition, the brain strengthens the neural circuits associated with perseverance and discipline, making it easier to engage in challenging tasks over time.

Daily habits are essential to this process. These habits, such as setting small, achievable goals, practicing mindfulness to regulate stress, and engaging in deliberate cold exposure or exercise, can enhance dopamine release—a neurochemical that promotes motivation and reward-seeking behavior. Dopamine not only fuels the desire to achieve but also helps sustain effort during difficult or prolonged tasks.

Here are some practical exercises to help you cultivate grit:

1. **Daily Reflection:** Spend a few minutes each day reflecting on your progress, challenges, and areas for improvement. Journaling can be a helpful tool for this practice. Write about what you achieved, what obstacles you faced, and how you overcame them. This habit reinforces your commitment and highlights your resilience.

2. **Set Micro-Goals:** Establish small, achievable goals each day. Completing these tasks will provide a sense of accomplishment and motivation to keep going. These micro-goals could be as simple as reading a book chapter, finishing a short workout, or making a positive step towards a larger goal.

3. **Practice Mindfulness:** Incorporate mindfulness techniques, such as meditation or deep breathing exercises, to enhance focus and reduce stress. Mindfulness helps you stay present and maintain a clear, calm mind, essential for overcoming challenges and staying focused on your goals.

4. **Exercise Regularly:** Physical activity boosts mental resilience and overall well-being. Aim for at least 30 minutes of exercise most days of the week. Regular exercise improves physical health and enhances mental clarity and emotional stability.

5. **Read Inspirational Stories:** Learn from the experiences of others who have demonstrated grit and resilience. Their stories can provide valuable insights and motivation. Books, podcasts, and documentaries about individuals who have overcome significant challenges can be particularly inspiring.

6. **Build a Routine:** Establish a daily routine incorporating time for goal-related activities, self-care, and relaxation. A structured routine helps you stay disciplined and ensures that you allocate time for the activities that matter most.

7. **Find Community and Connection:** Seek and surround oneself with others who share similar goals and values fosters a sense of belonging that make It easier to persist In the face of adversity.

ADDITIONAL PRACTICES FOR BUILDING GRIT

1. **Embrace Failure:** Redefine failure as a learning opportunity. Each failure provides insights that bring you closer to success. Reflect on your failures and identify what you can do differently next time.

2. **Visualize Success:** Spend a few minutes each day visualizing your goals' successful achievement. This mental rehearsal can increase motivation and help you focus on your long-term vision.

3. **Develop Self-Compassion:** Treat yourself with kindness and understanding, especially when facing difficulties. Self-compassion helps you recover from setbacks more quickly and maintain a positive outlook.

4. **Cultivate Patience:** Understand that building grit and achieving long-term goals takes time. Practice patience by focusing on the process rather than the outcome. Celebrate small wins along the way to maintain motivation.

5. **Seek Serenity:** Know that there are things you cannot control and be able to accept those things. Finding serenity and peace with those things helps you build the inner calm for a focused mind and less stress, enhancing your ability to preserve.

Grit is not something we are born with; it's a skill that we can develop and refine over time, much like any other neural or physical adaptation. The science behind grit is tied deeply to the concept of neuroplasticity—the brain's ability to change and adapt based on our experiences, efforts, and focus.

To cultivate grit, one of the most powerful frameworks we can utilize is the development of a *growth mindset*. This term, originally coined by Dr. Carol Dweck, refers to the belief that abilities and intelligence can be developed through hard work, strategy, and feedback. When you adopt a growth mindset, you view challenges not as threats, but as opportunities for development, and this rewires the brain to engage more fully with difficult tasks rather than shy away from them.

Setting clear, long-term goals is also critical. There's neuroscience to support that when we set meaningful and challenging goals, especially those aligned with our deeper values and purpose, we engage the brain's dopaminergic reward system. This system is essential for motivation and perseverance because it reinforces our efforts and makes the pursuit of those goals intrinsically satisfying. It's this sustained engagement of the reward system that contributes to the long-term development of grit.

When it comes to overcoming obstacles, resilience is key, and from a neurological standpoint, resilience can be understood as the capacity to manage stress and recover from setbacks. Stress is inevitable when pursuing challenging goals, but with resilience training—such as mindfulness, structured stress exposure, and cognitive reframing—we can optimize our brain's response to stress. Studies show that when we interpret stress as a sign of growth or learning, the prefrontal cortex (responsible for planning and decision-making) remains more engaged, allowing us to think clearly and maintain focus, even under pressure.

Incorporating practical exercises to build grit involves deliberate practice—working on tasks just beyond your current ability—and what neuroscientists call "deep focus" or "flow." This is when the brain is highly engaged in a specific task, producing both challenge and skill enhancement.

Regularly engaging in focused, deliberate practice, along with rest and recovery, enables the brain to strengthen its neural connections, promoting both resilience and persistence in the face of difficulty.

Ultimately, grit is a neural trait built over time, with consistent effort and dedication. By adopting a growth mindset, setting purposeful goals, building resilience, and engaging in targeted, practical exercises, we can literally reshape the brain to become more adaptable and persistent. This, in turn, allows us to overcome adversity and achieve our most ambitious aspirations.

4

Practicing Gratitude

In the fast pace and often repetitive nature of our daily lives, it becomes easy to overlook the subtle yet profound experiences that ground us and contribute to our well-being. But, from a neurobiological perspective, gratitude plays a far more significant role than we might think. Gratitude is not merely about being thankful; it's a practice that alters our brain chemistry, enhancing neural circuits involved in social bonding, emotional regulation, and resilience.

Neuroscientific research has shown that gratitude activates the brain's reward systems, particularly the release of dopamine and serotonin—neurotransmitters essential for feelings of happiness and contentment. Over time, this repeated activation strengthens neural pathways that allow us to notice and appreciate positive experiences more easily, even amid adversity. This is especially critical during stressful or challenging times when the brain is often primed to focus on potential threats or negative outcomes.

In this chapter, we'll dive into the mechanisms behind how practicing gratitude reshapes the brain and its implications for mental and emotional health. We'll explore how this simple yet powerful practice can not only uplift our own lives but also foster a ripple effect, positively influencing the mood and behavior of those around us through social contagion. Additionally, we'll examine several practical, neuroscience-backed exercises—like gratitude journaling, reframing, and mindful reflection—that can help cultivate a more grateful mindset. These practices can enhance your ability to shift focus from stressors to resources, fostering a more resilient, optimistic outlook in the long term.

Gratitude, therefore, is not just a fleeting emotional response but a strategic tool for enhancing mental health, optimizing social relationships, and maintaining balance in an ever-demanding world.

DAILY GRATITUDE PRACTICES AND ROUTINES

Every morning, as the sun peeks over the horizon, setting the world aglow with its warm light, we are given an opportunity to start our day with gratitude. Establishing daily gratitude practices can be a powerful way to anchor ourselves, no matter what lies ahead.

Morning Gratitude Journaling: Begin your day by jotting down three things you are grateful for. These can be as simple as the comforting aroma of your morning coffee, birds chirping outside your window, or the support of a loved one. Focusing on positive aspects sets a hopeful and appreciative tone for the day.

Gratitude Jar: Keep a jar on your desk or kitchen counter. Daily, write down a moment of gratitude on a slip of paper and drop it into the jar. Over time, watching the jar fill up with these notes becomes a tangible reminder of the abundance in your life.

Mindful Moments: Integrate gratitude into your daily routines. Whether it's during your morning shower, your commute, or your evening wind-down, take a moment to reflect on something you appreciate about your life or the world around you.

Research by Emmons and McCullough (2003) in their study "Counting Blessings Versus Burdens: An Experimental Investigation of Gratitude and Subjective Well-Being in Daily Life" found that individuals who kept a weekly gratitude journal reported fewer physical symptoms, felt better about their lives, and were more optimistic about the upcoming week compared to those who recorded hassles or neutral life events.

CULTIVATING GRATITUDE IN CHALLENGING TIMES

In life, we are all inevitably faced with challenges—some that shake us to our core. It's in these moments of adversity that our resilience is truly tested. The brain, under stress, tends to narrow its focus to negative stimuli, a natural response designed for survival. However, neuroscience shows us that we can intervene in this process through intentional practices, such as gratitude.

Gratitude, despite seeming counterintuitive during hardship, has profound effects on our brain's chemistry. Research suggests that when we actively engage in gratitude, we shift brain activity away from areas associated with fear and stress (such as the amygdala) and toward regions that promote positive emotion and well-being, like the prefrontal cortex. This rewiring enables us to break free from the brain's tendency to dwell on negative experiences, thus fostering a more adaptive and resilient mindset.

It's important to recognize that gratitude is not about dismissing challenges or pretending everything is fine. Rather, it is about anchoring the mind to something positive—something that fosters an internal state of safety and calm. When we practice gratitude, even in the storm, we harness neuroplasticity to reframe our perception of the situation, promoting psychological flexibility and long-term emotional health.

The ability to do this, particularly during times of stress, is like strengthening a muscle. Initially, it might feel difficult, even unnatural. But over time, and with consistent practice, gratitude becomes a powerful tool for regulating our emotional states and enhancing our capacity for resilience.

To approach challenging times while keeping gratitude at the core, we need to understand how our brain and nervous system respond to stress, as well as how practices like gratitude can fundamentally shift our neurochemistry to promote resilience and well-being.

REGULATING YOUR NERVOUS SYSTEM

When we're faced with adversity, our brain and body activate stress responses that are essential for survival. However, chronic stress can lead to dysregulation of the autonomic nervous system, particularly the sympathetic branch (responsible for fight-or-flight). To counteract this, we can engage in activities that promote parasympathetic activation (rest and digest), which helps us return to a balanced state.

- **Breathwork**: One of the most effective tools is deliberate breathwork. Slow, controlled breathing, significantly extending the exhale longer than the inhale, can signal to the brain that it's safe to downshift from a stress state. Practices such as box breathing (inhale for 4 seconds, hold for 4, exhale for 4, and hold for 4) can promote this shift, activating the parasympathetic nervous system.
- **Physical Movement**: Engaging in moderate-intensity aerobic exercise can reduce the levels of cortisol (a stress hormone) and improve mood by increasing dopamine and serotonin, which are crucial for motivation and emotional stability. Exercise also helps to release endorphins, which act as natural painkillers and mood elevators.

SHIFTING YOUR PERSPECTIVE

Neuroplasticity, or the brain's ability to reorganize and form new neural connections, means that the brain can adapt to new patterns of thought and behavior even during challenging times. Gratitude is a potent tool in rewiring our brain's response to adversity.

- **Gratitude Practice and Neurochemical Shifts**: Research has shown that regularly practicing gratitude can increase the production of neurotransmitters like dopamine and serotonin, which play a key role in creating feelings of well-being and hope. Gratitude also impacts the brain's reward circuits by increasing activity in the prefrontal cortex, helping us focus on positive aspects of life, even in difficult moments.

- **Journaling**: One way to activate these systems is to engage in reflective practices, such as gratitude journaling. Writing down three to five things you are grateful for every day can shift attention from stressors to positives, which primes the brain to notice opportunities and solutions. Over time, this shifts neural circuits, increasing emotional resilience.

THE ROLE OF SOCIAL CONNECTION

When we are navigating difficult times, isolation can often exacerbate the stress response. Oxytocin, sometimes referred to as the "bonding hormone," is released during social interactions and helps mitigate the effects of stress on the body. Strengthening social ties is essential for emotional recovery during hardship.

- **Deep Conversations**: Engage in meaningful conversations with friends, family, or colleagues. Authentic connection helps to activate brain circuits tied to trust, cooperation, and emotional support, all of which reduce stress and help you process difficult emotions in a healthier way.
- **Offering Support**: It's interesting to note that the act of giving support, not just receiving it, triggers the release of oxytocin. This has been shown to lower stress and enhance feelings of gratitude, creating a feedback loop that reinforces emotional resilience.

LEVERAGING THE POWER OF SLEEP AND RECOVERY

Challenging times often disturb sleep, which in turn exacerbates stress and reduces our ability to manage emotions. The brain uses sleep to recover and consolidate emotional memories, making sleep crucial for overcoming adversity.

- **Sleep and Neuroplasticity**: Sleep is when much of neuroplasticity occurs, meaning the brain reorganizes and processes the day's emotional experiences. Deep sleep, in particular, aids in the consolidation of positive emotional memories, while also helping to prune away negative emotional responses tied to the day's events.

- **Sleep Optimization**: Prioritize 7-9 hours of quality sleep by creating a consistent sleep schedule and reducing blue light exposure before bedtime. Practices like meditation or mindfulness before sleep can calm the nervous system, making it easier to fall into restorative sleep.

GROWTH THROUGH GRATITUDE: SHIFTING FROM A FIXED TO A GROWTH MINDSET

One of the key psychological shifts during challenging times is moving from a fixed mindset, where difficulties are seen as insurmountable, to a growth mindset, where challenges are seen as opportunities for development. Gratitude fosters this shift by reminding the brain of past successes, the resources available to us, and the inherent potential for change.

- **Gratitude and Resilience**: Neuroimaging studies suggest that gratitude not only enhances mood but also improves cognitive flexibility, making it easier to adopt a growth mindset. By training the brain to focus on what is going well, we prepare it to be more adaptive, which is crucial for overcoming setbacks.
- **Affirming Progress**: Acknowledge even small wins throughout your day. This practice reinforces the neuroplastic changes associated with resilience, helping the brain become more attuned to progress and potential growth.

By integrating these practices, we harness the brain's ability to adapt and grow, even under stress, while keeping gratitude as the anchor that shapes our emotional response to life's challenges.

THE RIPPLE EFFECT: HOW GRATITUDE INFLUENCES OTHERS

Gratitude is not just a simple emotion; it's a powerful neurobiological tool that can profoundly shape human behavior and communities. When we express gratitude, it activates the brain's reward circuits, particularly involving the neurotransmitter dopamine, which makes us feel good and drives us to seek more of the same. This is why gratitude is inherently contagious. When one person expresses genuine appreciation, it has a ripple effect—triggering a neurochemical response in the recipient that often compels them to pass that gratitude on to others. This dynamic can significantly transform individual mindsets, interpersonal relationships, and even entire organizations and communities.

IN THE WORKPLACE

In work environments, gratitude acts as a social glue that fosters trust, motivation, and collaboration. When a manager consistently acknowledges the efforts and achievements of their team, they are not merely boosting morale; they are actually promoting a neurochemical environment where team members feel psychologically safe and motivated to perform better. The brain's dopamine and oxytocin systems—key players in reward, bonding, and social connection—are activated, leading to improved interpersonal dynamics.

Employees who feel genuinely appreciated are more likely to engage in prosocial behavior, helping colleagues, going the extra mile, and maintaining a positive attitude under pressure. A culture of gratitude is not just about being nice; it's about creating a workplace where the neurobiology of each individual is aligned with collective goals. Research by Waters (2012) has shown that gratitude interventions, such as keeping gratitude journals or fostering regular expressions of thanks, lead to marked improvements in job satisfaction and emotional well-being. Such practices also correlate with lower burnout rates and better workplace cohesion. Gratitude, then, is an invaluable tool for leaders who want to create high-functioning, resilient teams.

In Personal Relationships

On a personal level, gratitude strengthens emotional bonds and deepens intimacy. When you express appreciation toward a partner, friend, or family member, you're essentially tapping into the brain's oxytocin system, which enhances feelings of trust and connection. This neurochemical feedback loop is what makes simple acts of appreciation—like thanking someone for their support or recognizing their kindness—so impactful. It not only makes the other person feel valued, but also reinforces the relationship's emotional foundation.

According to research by Algoe, Gable, and Maisel (2010), partners who regularly express gratitude toward each other experience greater relationship satisfaction and emotional stability. This is because gratitude promotes a cycle of positive reinforcement, where both partners feel more inclined to engage in supportive behaviors, leading to greater long-term relationship health.

In the Community

At a broader societal level, gratitude acts as a key driver for community-building. When gratitude is expressed toward service workers, volunteers, or even local businesses, it reinforces social bonds and cultivates a sense of shared responsibility. This is, in part, due to the neurobiology of social connection: when people feel appreciated, they're more likely to reciprocate and engage with their community in meaningful ways. Acts of gratitude can inspire a ripple effect, where more people feel inclined to contribute positively, creating a feedback loop that strengthens the social fabric.

In a community context, gratitude does more than just make people feel good—it serves as a catalyst for collective well-being. When people recognize the contributions of others, they enhance the cooperative dynamics within that community, making it more resilient and cohesive.

In essence, gratitude, as neuroscience shows, is far more than a nicety—it's a tool for building stronger connections, fostering healthier workplaces, and creating more supportive communities. Whether in the workplace, in personal relationships, or in society at large, gratitude has a profound, ripple-like effect that is grounded in our biology.

PRACTICAL EXERCISES TO ENHANCE GRATITUDE

To truly understand the science of gratitude and how it can deeply impact your brain, body, and overall well-being, it's crucial to move beyond the concept and engage in deliberate, consistent practices that stimulate neuroplasticity—the brain's ability to change and reorganize itself. By engaging in gratitude exercises, you are not just feeling better emotionally; you're literally rewiring your brain to focus on positivity and resilience. Let's delve into a few science-based practices that can help you cultivate gratitude and explain why they work.

GRATITUDE WALKS

Taking a gratitude walk is a powerful way to combine movement with intentional thought, enhancing both physical and mental well-being. Research shows that physical activity increases neurogenesis, the process by which new neurons are created in the brain. When you pair this with gratitude reflections, you're not only boosting your cardiovascular health but also activating neural circuits associated with positive emotions, particularly in the prefrontal cortex and the anterior cingulate cortex. As you walk, take in your surroundings—the rustle of leaves, the warmth of the sun, or even the rhythmic sound of your footsteps. Let your awareness of these small details reinforce your sense of connection to the world around you. This practice engages your brain's reward systems, particularly the release of dopamine, a key neurotransmitter involved in feelings of pleasure and satisfaction.

GRATITUDE LETTERS

The act of writing a gratitude letter taps into the brain's social bonding and reward systems, specifically areas like the ventral tegmental area (VTA) and the striatum, which are associated with the release of oxytocin, the "bonding hormone." By recalling specific instances where someone positively impacted your life, you're reinforcing neural pathways that associate human connection with well-being. Even if you don't send the letter, the process itself has been shown to elevate mood and improve long-term mental health. A seminal study by Seligman et al. (2005) found that individuals who wrote and delivered gratitude letters experienced a significant increase in happiness, and this effect lasted for over a month. The act of reflection in this case strengthens memory consolidation around positive experiences, helping to create a default mindset of appreciation.

Mindful Breathing

Mindful breathing, paired with gratitude, engages both the parasympathetic nervous system (rest-and-digest) and the prefrontal cortex, which helps regulate emotions and reduces reactivity to stress. When you focus on your breath, particularly extending your exhale, you activate the vagus nerve, which has calming effects on the body. By intentionally pairing each breath with thoughts of gratitude, you're creating a powerful feedback loop. Inhalation brings to mind something or someone you're grateful for, stimulating brain regions associated with positive emotions. As you exhale, you're practicing letting go of negative emotions, a process that can reduce levels of cortisol, the stress hormone, over time. This combination enhances emotional regulation and strengthens your ability to maintain a positive outlook, even under stress.

Gratitude Visualizations

Visualization is a powerful mental tool that involves engaging your brain's sensory and emotional circuits. When you visualize a moment where you felt truly grateful, you are activating the same neural pathways as if you were reliving the experience in real time. This can stimulate the hippocampus, which is crucial for memory and emotional regulation, and the ventromedial prefrontal cortex, which is associated with long-term emotional well-being. The act of vividly imagining these moments brings up associated feelings of gratitude, creating a feedback loop that strengthens neural connections involved in positive emotions. This practice not only increases feelings of appreciation but also helps solidify a neural baseline of gratitude, making it easier to access these feelings in the future.

THE SCIENCE OF GRATITUDE AS A DAILY PRACTICE

Practicing gratitude is not simply about momentary happiness; it's about training your brain to focus on positive experiences and emotions. The brain has a negativity bias—it naturally scans for threats or problems—an evolutionary mechanism that has kept humans alive. However, this bias can be rebalanced through intentional practices like gratitude, which create new neural pathways that prioritize positive emotions and reduce stress. Over time, the regular practice of gratitude changes your brain's wiring, making you more resilient, optimistic, and better equipped to deal with challenges.

By engaging in these practices regularly, especially during difficult periods, you are strengthening your brain's capacity to experience sustained gratitude and joy. This not only enhances your own mental health but can also have a profound ripple effect on others, fostering a deeper sense of connection, kindness, and appreciation within your social network. Gratitude has the potential to transform not just individual lives but the broader culture of relationships and communities.

5

Grit and Gratitude in the Workplace

Grit and gratitude are not just abstract qualities; they are competencies rooted in neurobiological processes, and they manifest as measurable sets of behaviors. When properly understood and cultivated, they can significantly enhance performance, resilience, and social dynamics in the workplace.

GRIT: THE NEUROSCIENCE OF SUSTAINED EFFORT

Grit, as defined by Angela Duckworth, is the ability to maintain effort and passion for long-term goals. From a neuroscientific perspective, grit is tightly linked to the brain's reward systems, particularly involving dopamine, which is essential for motivation and persistence.

Dopamine plays a crucial role in goal-directed behavior. It's not simply released when we achieve a goal, but rather, it surges when we pursue difficult challenges, helping to keep us engaged. This is a critical mechanism in how grit operates: individuals who demonstrate high levels of grit have developed the ability to reframe challenges as opportunities for growth, which keeps their dopamine systems engaged. This process drives them forward despite setbacks and failures.

In the workplace, grit is observable in employees who consistently pursue long-term objectives, even when faced with obstacles. It manifests in their ability to recover from failure, adapt to new strategies, and maintain focus on larger goals despite immediate setbacks. Interestingly, studies show that individuals with higher levels of grit tend to have thicker gray matter in brain regions like the anterior cingulate cortex (ACC) and prefrontal cortex, areas responsible for decision-making, impulse control, and emotional regulation.

GRATITUDE: WIRING THE BRAIN FOR SOCIAL COHESION AND WELL-BEING

Gratitude, on the other hand, operates in a different but complementary neural circuit. While grit is primarily about maintaining effort toward personal goals, gratitude enhances social bonding and well-being, key factors in workplace environments where collaboration and trust are crucial.

When we experience or express gratitude, the brain releases a cascade of neurotransmitters such as oxytocin and serotonin, which foster feelings of trust, connection, and happiness. This is vital for creating positive social dynamics at work. Employees who regularly engage in gratitude practices are more likely to form strong, cooperative relationships with colleagues, leading to improved team performance and reduced burnout.

From a neurobiological perspective, gratitude helps modulate stress responses by activating brain regions like the ventromedial prefrontal cortex (vmPFC), which is involved in emotional regulation and perspective-taking. This ability to see challenges through a broader, more positive lens can reduce workplace anxiety and improve overall job satisfaction.

To fully leverage the benefits of grit and gratitude in the workplace, it's essential to recognize that these qualities are not innate talents but rather competencies—sets of behaviors and skills that can be cultivated, refined, and strategically applied to enhance both individual and organizational performance.

GRIT COMPETENCY

Grit is the ability to demonstrate passion, perseverance, and resilience to pursue long-term goals, despite obstacles and challenges.

KEY BEHAVIORS:

1. **Goal-oriented**: Sets clear, challenging goals and prioritizes efforts to achieve them.
2. **Resilient**: Bounces back from setbacks, failures, and disappointments.
3. **Determined**: Maintains focus and motivation, even when faced with obstacles.
4. **Hardworking**: Puts in the time and effort required to achieve goals.
5. **Adaptable**: Adjusts approach as needed, learning from failures and setbacks.
6. **Passionate**: Demonstrates enthusiasm and commitment to goals and interests.
7. **Self-disciplined**: Manages time, emotions, and behaviors to focus on goals.

GRATITUDE COMPETENCY

Gratitude is recognizing, appreciating, and expressing thanks for the positive aspects of life, relationships, and experiences.

KEY BEHAVIORS:

1. **Aware**: Recognizes and acknowledges the good things in life.
2. **Appreciative**: Values and cherishes the people, experiences, and circumstances that bring joy.
3. **Thankful**: Expresses gratitude through words, actions, or gestures.
4. **Positive**: Focuses on the good rather than dwelling on the negative.
5. **Reflective**: Consider and appreciate the blessings and benefits received.
6. **Generous**: Shows appreciation through acts of kindness and generosity.
7. **Humility**: Acknowledges the role of others and circumstances in one's life and success.

By developing these competencies, individuals, leaders, and organizations can cultivate a growth mindset, build stronger relationships, and achieve greater success and well-being.

THE IMPACT ON EMPLOYEE ENGAGEMENT AND PRODUCTIVITY

With its rapid changes and relentless pace, the modern workplace demands not just technical skills but also a unique blend of personal qualities from employees—grit and gratitude. These traits, often overlooked, are pivotal in driving employee engagement and productivity. Grit, defined as perseverance and passion for long-term goals, helps employees push through challenges, maintain focus, and achieve excellence. Gratitude, on the other hand, fosters a positive work environment, enhancing morale and collaboration.

SCHOLARLY RESEARCH ON GRIT AND GRATITUDE

Angela Duckworth's seminal research on grit defines it as a combination of passion and perseverance for long-term goals. Her studies have shown that grit significantly predicts success, often more so than talent or intelligence. Duckworth's Grit Scale, used to measure an individual's grit, has been validated across diverse populations and contexts, underscoring the importance of this trait in various fields, including the workplace.

On the other hand, gratitude has been extensively studied in positive psychology. Research by Dr. Robert Emmons, one of the leading scholars on gratitude, indicates that practicing gratitude can enhance well-being, improve relationships, and increase resilience. Emmons' work demonstrates that gratitude can lead to higher psychological and physical well-being levels, which translates into increased productivity and engagement at work.

IMPACT ON EMPLOYEE ENGAGEMENT AND PRODUCTIVITY

Engaged employees are deeply involved in, enthusiastic about, and committed to their work. When grit is part of the workplace culture, employees are more likely to stay committed despite obstacles. They see challenges as opportunities to grow rather than insurmountable problems. This mindset leads to higher productivity as employees strive to achieve their goals with determination and resilience.

Gratitude complements grit by creating a supportive and appreciative work atmosphere. When employees feel valued and recognized, their motivation and satisfaction levels soar. This positive reinforcement encourages them to go the extra mile, knowing their efforts are acknowledged and appreciated. The combination of grit and gratitude thus forms a powerful duo that significantly boosts employee engagement and productivity.

STRATEGIES FOR LEADERS TO FOSTER A CULTURE OF GRIT AND GRATITUDE

When we think about the neuroscience behind fostering a culture of grit and gratitude, it's essential to understand how our brains function under stress, reward, and recognition. Leaders, whether they realize it or not, play a critical role in shaping not only workplace behaviors but also the neural circuitry of their teams. From a neuroscience perspective, cultivating grit and gratitude taps into brain pathways that govern motivation, resilience, and social bonding.

Here are key strategies, infused with deeper context around neurobiology, to help leaders foster a culture of grit and gratitude in the workplace:

MODEL THE BEHAVIOR: SET NEURAL PATTERNS FOR RESILIENCE

Leaders who exhibit grit and gratitude influence the mirror neurons of their employees. Mirror neurons help us mimic and internalize the behaviors we see in others, so when leaders consistently demonstrate persever-ance in challenging situations, they model a neural pathway of resilience for the team. Similarly, when leaders express genuine gratitude, it activates the brain's reward systems in both the giver and receiver, promoting a more positive and motivated workplace.

Application Tip: Persevering in the face of challenges recruits areas of the brain such as the prefrontal cortex (involved in planning and decision-making) and the anterior cingulate cortex (which regulates emotions and error detection). Leaders who maintain their composure during adversity help their teams strengthen these brain regions by observation and imitation.

PROVIDE RESOURCES AND SUPPORT: ACTIVATE LEARNING AND GROWTH CIRCUITS

When employees have access to tools, training, and support, you are engaging their dopaminergic reward system, specifically the pathways involved in anticipation and achievement. Mentorship and resilience training allow individuals to push through difficult tasks, strengthening their prefrontal cortex, the brain's command center for grit. Furthermore, offering support encourages the release of oxytocin, the bonding hormone, creating a sense of safety and connection within the team.

Application Tip: Resilience is often a reflection of one's ability to predict success after effort. Dopamine surges not just when we achieve a goal but when we anticipate progress, so providing pathways for growth helps maintain motivation.

RECOGNIZE AND CELEBRATE EFFORTS: REINFORCE POSITIVE DOPAMINE LOOPS

Recognition is one of the most effective ways to trigger the brain's reward system. Positive feedback, when delivered immediately following an accomplishment, helps reinforce neural pathways associated with success. Celebrating team and individual wins helps to amplify the brain's release of dopamine, which reinforces the desire to continue putting in effort and builds a strong feedback loop between effort and reward.

Application Tip: Dopamine spikes are greater when rewards are unpredictable. By offering timely and varied forms of recognition, leaders can maintain high levels of employee motivation and engagement.

ENCOURAGE A GROWTH MINDSET: REWIRE NEURAL CONNECTIONS FOR ADAPTABILITY

A growth mindset is grounded in neuroplasticity, the brain's ability to reorganize itself by forming new neural connections throughout life. By encouraging employees to see mistakes as opportunities for learning, leaders help their teams reframe failure and engage their hippocampus, which is involved in learning and memory. This creates a feedback loop where employees become more resilient to setbacks because their brains are literally rewiring themselves for adaptability.

Application Tip: The brain's plasticity allows it to change based on experience. Leaders can capitalize on this by promoting environments where trying new things, even at the risk of failure, is seen as essential for learning and growth.

FOSTER A SUPPORTIVE COMMUNITY: ENHANCE OXYTOCIN AND COLLECTIVE RESILIENCE

Humans are inherently social creatures, and our brains are wired to thrive in supportive environments. Team-building activities and peer recognition boost the release of oxytocin, which fosters trust and social bonding. By creating a sense of community, leaders can enhance their team's ability to persevere through challenges, knowing that they have a network of support.

Application Tip: Oxytocin not only helps in bonding but also reduces stress by dampening the activity of the amygdala, the brain's fear center. A supportive community can mitigate stress responses and build resilience.

SOLICIT AND ACT ON FEEDBACK: STRENGTHEN TRUST AND ENGAGEMENT

Regular feedback taps into the brain's reward circuitry, particularly when feedback leads to tangible improvements. The act of listening and responding to employee input triggers trust-building mechanisms in the brain, engaging the ventromedial prefrontal cortex, which is associated with decision-making and social trust.

Application Tip: Feedback is most effective when it's constructive and actionable. Leaders who incorporate employee feedback into decision-making create a culture where team members feel valued, enhancing overall neural engagement in problem-solving and innovation.

RECOGNIZE AND REWARD EFFORT: CREATE A BALANCE OF IMMEDIATE AND LONG-TERM REWARD SYSTEMS

Recognizing effort, not just results, activates both short-term reward systems (through dopamine release) and long-term reward systems (through serotonin regulation). By rewarding persistence and progress, leaders help employees build resilience as they experience consistent, incremental rewards for their hard work.

Application Tip: Acknowledging effort leverages both the mesolimbic pathway (associated with immediate rewards) and the serotoninergic system (linked to mood stabilization and long-term contentment). This balance supports both motivation and well-being.

PROMOTE POSITIVITY AND APPRECIATION: ENHANCE THE BRAIN'S GRATITUDE NETWORK

Practicing gratitude has been shown to activate brain regions like the ventromedial prefrontal cortex, associated with reward, and the hypothalamus, which regulates emotions and stress. When leaders encourage gratitude practices—whether it's through sharing appreciation or recognizing milestones—they are strengthening these networks, reducing stress, and fostering a more positive emotional climate.

Application Tip: Gratitude practice enhances well-being and increases prosocial behavior by boosting serotonin and oxytocin. A culture of gratitude helps individuals feel valued and encourages further acts of kindness and perseverance.

EMPHASIZE PURPOSE AND MEANING: ACTIVATE THE BRAIN'S LONG-TERM MOTIVATION CIRCUITS

Purpose and meaning are critical drivers of long-term engagement. Offering development opportunities, aligning individual goals with organizational missions, and fostering a sense of purpose tap into the brain's intrinsic motivation systems, specifically involving the ventral striatum, a key player in long-term goal setting and achievement.

Application Tip: When individuals find meaning in their work, they engage the brain's eudaimonic pathways, which are linked to long-lasting satisfaction, as opposed to hedonic short-term pleasure. Purpose fuels grit by giving employees a "why" behind their efforts.

Incorporating these strategies not only fosters grit and gratitude in the workplace but also aligns with how the brain naturally functions under the right conditions of motivation, support, and recognition. Leaders who understand these principles are not just improving performance but are also helping their employees build the neural resilience required for long-term success.

TIPS FOR EMPLOYEES TO INTEGRATE GRIT AND GRATITUDE INTO THEIR WORK LIFE

Integrating grit and gratitude into one's work life isn't just about pushing through challenges or being polite—it's about leveraging neuroscience and psychology to rewire our brains for sustained motivation, focus, and well-being. Grit, as defined by psychologist Angela Duckworth, is the perseverance and passion for long-term goals, while gratitude is the practice of recognizing and appreciating the positive aspects of life. Both are critical for optimal performance and mental health. Here's a more in-depth look at how employees can cultivate these traits, framed through a neuroscience-informed lens.

Set Clear, Attainable Goals:

From a neurobiological standpoint, goal setting triggers the release of dopamine, a neurotransmitter tied to motivation and reward. Dopamine is most effective when goals are specific and challenging yet attainable. To build grit, employees should break down long-term objectives into smaller, manageable milestones. This gradual progression gives your brain more frequent dopamine rewards, reinforcing persistence and helping you maintain focus over the long term.

Tip: Use daily rituals like journaling to map out your goals and review progress. Neuroplasticity—the brain's ability to reorganize itself—occurs most effectively when the brain has time to reflect and consolidate new information.

Practice Self-Care:

Grit often evokes images of relentless effort, but research shows that effective grit requires oscillation between intense focus and deliberate rest. Burnout disrupts the brain's prefrontal cortex, which is crucial for decision-making, problem-solving, and emotional regulation. To prevent this, employees need to practice self-care routines that optimize brain health, including regular sleep, exercise, and mindfulness practices.

Neuroscience has shown that exercise boosts neurogenesis (the creation of new neurons), which helps improve mood and cognitive function. Meanwhile, mindfulness and meditation strengthen the brain's ability to focus, reduce stress, and promote resilience. This balance between work and recovery is essential for sustained grit.

Tip: Incorporate micro-breaks during your workday to reset your mental focus, even if it's just for 5 minutes of deep breathing.

EXPRESS GRATITUDE REGULARLY:

Gratitude isn't just a feel-good practice—scientific studies show it has measurable effects on the brain. When you express gratitude, your brain releases serotonin and dopamine, which enhance mood and increase feelings of connection and well-being. This helps reduce the brain's tendency to focus on stress and threats, promoting a more balanced and resilient mental state.

In the workplace, expressing gratitude to colleagues strengthens social bonds and creates a more supportive environment, fostering collaboration and mutual trust. Even small acts, like writing a note of appreciation, can amplify social cohesion and contribute to a more positive work culture.

Tip: Set aside time each day to reflect on three things you're grateful for, both at work and in life. This simple practice can retrain your brain to scan for positive experiences, reinforcing a more optimistic mindset.

SEEK SUPPORT AND COMMUNITY:

Humans are inherently social creatures, and neuroscience has shown that social support is crucial in reducing stress and promoting well-being. Building a network of supportive colleagues can enhance your resilience, providing both emotional and professional support during difficult times. Moreover, a sense of belonging and connection releases oxytocin, a hormone that reduces the stress response and enhances feelings of trust.

Tip: Foster relationships by actively participating in team activities, engaging in mentorship opportunities, and being vulnerable about challenges when appropriate.

REFLECT AND CELEBRATE SMALL WINS:

Grit isn't about grinding endlessly; it's about recognizing progress and using those moments as fuel to keep going. Regular reflection activates the brain's reward circuitry, reinforcing positive behaviors and keeping motivation high. Celebrating even small wins creates a positive feedback loop in the brain, boosting confidence and resilience.

Tip: After completing a challenging task, take a moment to reflect on the effort you invested. Documenting these victories can strengthen the neural pathways associated with achievement, making it easier to persevere in future challenges.

REFRAME CHALLENGES AS LEARNING OPPORTUNITIES:

Neuroscience shows that reframing how you perceive challenges can significantly alter how your brain processes stress. Instead of viewing obstacles as threats, view them as opportunities for growth. This mindset activates the brain's learning centers, such as the hippocampus, and reduces the activity of the amygdala, which is responsible for fear and anxiety. By reframing challenges, you shift from a state of anxiety to one of curiosity and learning.

Tip: When faced with a setback, ask yourself, "What can I learn from this?" This primes your brain to adapt and grow, rather than retreat in the face of difficulty.

SEEK ROLE MODELS:

Research shows that having a role model who embodies the qualities you want to develop—such as grit and gratitude—activates the brain's mirror neurons, which are responsible for learning through observation. When you regularly engage with people who demonstrate resilience and positivity, your brain adopts similar behaviors.

Tip: Identify mentors or colleagues who display these qualities and seek regular interactions with them. Pay attention not just to what they do, but how they think and approach challenges.

CONNECT WITH NATURE:

Spending time in nature has profound effects on brain function. Studies have shown that time outdoors reduces cortisol levels (a stress hormone), improves cognitive performance, and enhances creativity. Nature exposure also activates areas of the brain associated with calm and focus, helping to reset after long periods of work.

Tip: Incorporate "green breaks" into your routine, such as walking outside during lunch or working near a window with natural light. This helps maintain mental clarity and emotional balance.

By integrating these practices, employees not only build their mental toughness (grit) but also foster a deep sense of connection, positivity, and well-being (gratitude). Through regular reflection, community-building, and self-care, the brain becomes better equipped to handle adversity, achieve goals, and maintain long-term success.

Grit and gratitude are transformative traits that can significantly enhance employee engagement and productivity. Organizations can create a more motivated, resilient, and satisfied workforce by fostering a culture that values perseverance and appreciation. Leaders play a crucial role in modeling these behaviors and implementing strategies that support their development. Employees can also integrate grit and gratitude into their daily work life, contributing to a positive and productive workplace environment. Together, these efforts can lead to sustained success and a thriving organizational culture.

6

Grit and Gratitude in Relationships

In the intricate landscape of human relationships, two qualities—grit and gratitude—serve as cornerstones for resilience, growth, and deep connection. Grit, the relentless pursuit of long-term goals despite obstacles and setbacks, often manifests as the commitment to endure the ups and downs of partnerships, friendships, and family ties. It's the ability to stay emotionally engaged even when conflicts arise or the road seems uncertain. On the other hand, gratitude—our recognition of the positive aspects within our relationships—provides the emotional nourishment needed to sustain that grit. Gratitude allows us to appreciate not only the high points but also the quiet, everyday moments that strengthen our bonds over time.

When paired together, grit and gratitude form a powerful dynamic that can transform relationships. Grit keeps us in the game during difficult times, while gratitude helps us focus on what's going right, fostering a sense of balance and fulfillment. In this chapter, we'll explore how these two forces work in tandem to create deeper, more meaningful connections. Drawing from research in psychology and neuroscience, we'll look at practical strategies to cultivate both grit and gratitude in our relationships, and how these traits can foster a sense of mutual growth, even in the face of conflict and adversity.

Much like the challenges of individual achievement, relationships require perseverance, patience, and a focus on long-term rewards. But while grit helps us push through the hard times, gratitude reminds us why it's worth it. Together, they create a foundation for lasting, authentic connections that can weather the storms and grow stronger as a result.

STRENGTHENING PERSONAL CONNECTIONS

The sound of laughter filled the room as Maya and James reminisced about their early days together. Sitting by the fireplace with a cup of tea, sharing stories that had become the foundation of their relationship was their favorite ritual.

Over the years, they had learned that personal connections are not built overnight but require constant nurturing and attention.

Strengthening personal connections begins with small, everyday actions. It's in the shared laughter, the whispered secrets, and the mutual support during tough times. It's about being present, truly listening, and showing up for each other consistently. Maya and James had their share of ups and downs, but what set them apart was their unwavering commitment to each other.

One evening, Maya noticed James seemed unusually quiet. Instead of brushing it off, she gently asked, "Is everything alright?" James hesitated but then opened up about the stress he was feeling at work. By creating a safe space for honest communication, Maya helped strengthen their bond. This openness and vulnerability are crucial in building deep, meaningful connections.

NAVIGATING CONFLICTS AND MAINTAINING HARMONY

Conflict is inevitable in any relationship, but it's how you navigate it that defines the strength of your bond. Maya and James had a rule: never go to bed angry. This simple guideline had saved them countless times. It forced them to confront their issues head-on and find solutions together.

One of their most memorable conflicts occurred during a family vacation. A misunderstanding escalated into a heated argument, and tensions ran high. But instead of letting the situation spiral out of control, they took a step back. They used a technique they had learned in a couples' workshop: active listening. Each person took turns speaking while the other listened without interrupting. It wasn't easy, but it allowed them to understand each other's perspectives and find common ground.

Maintaining harmony doesn't mean avoiding conflict altogether. It's about addressing issues with respect and empathy. It's recognizing that you're on the same team, even when you disagree. By approaching conflicts with a mindset of resolution rather than winning, Maya and James managed to maintain harmony in their relationship.

STORIES OF RESILIENCE AND APPRECIATION IN RELATIONSHIPS

Resilience in relationships often shines brightest during the darkest times. Maya and James faced a significant challenge when James was diagnosed with a serious illness. The news was devastating, and the future seemed uncertain. But instead of letting the situation pull them apart, they chose to face it together, with grit and gratitude.

Maya took on the role of caregiver, juggling her job and James's medical appointments. It was exhausting, both physically and emotionally. But every day, she reminded herself of the love they shared and the memories they had built. She practiced gratitude, focusing on the positive moments, no matter how small.

James, on the other hand, found strength in his appreciation for Maya. He realized the depth of her love and commitment, which fueled his determination to fight his illness. Together, they navigated this challenging journey, emerging stronger and more connected than ever.

Their story is a testament to the power of resilience and gratitude in relationships. By facing adversity with a positive attitude and unwavering support for each other, they turned a potentially relationship-breaking situation into a source of strength.

Another inspiring story comes from Lucy and Mark, who faced the challenge of long-distance due to Mark's job relocation. Initially, the distance strained their relationship, causing frequent misunderstandings and feelings of loneliness. However, they decided to focus on what they could control and made a conscious effort to stay connected. They scheduled regular video calls, sent handwritten letters, and planned visits as often as possible. Lucy and Mark's determination and appreciation for each other's efforts helped them overcome the distance, and they found that their relationship grew stronger as a result.

EXERCISES FOR COUPLES AND FAMILIES

To help other couples and families build grit and gratitude in their relationships, Maya and James developed a series of exercises based on their experiences:

1. **Gratitude Journal:** Each partner writes down three things they appreciate about the other daily. This exercise fosters positive feelings and reminds both partners of the good in their relationship.

2. **Active Listening Practice:** Set aside weekly time for a "listening session." One person speaks about their thoughts and feelings while the other listens attentively without interrupting. Then, switch roles. This practice enhances understanding and empathy.

3. **Conflict Resolution Steps:** Create a step-by-step plan for resolving conflicts. Include taking a break if emotions run high, using "I" statements to express feelings, and brainstorming solutions together.

4. **Quality Time Rituals:** Establish regular rituals for spending quality time together, such as a weekly date night, a daily walk, or a shared hobby. Consistent, intentional time together strengthens bonds.

5. **Support System Check-In:** Regularly check in with each other about your support systems. Discuss ways you can support each other better and identify external sources of support, such as friends, family, or counseling services.

6. **Resilience Building Activities:** Engage in activities that build resilience, such as physical exercise, mindfulness practices, and setting and achieving small goals together. These activities boost individual and collective strength.

7. **Appreciation Ritual:** At the end of each day, take a few minutes to share something you appreciate about each other. This ritual helps end the day on a positive note and reinforces gratitude.

8. **Future Planning Sessions:** Regularly discuss your goals and dreams for the future. Planning together helps to align your visions and fosters a sense of partnership and shared purpose.

9. **Family Meetings:** Hold regular family meetings where everyone can voice their thoughts and feelings. These meetings create an environment of open communication and mutual support.

10. **Mindful Touch:** Incorporate mindful touch, such as holding hands, hugs, or back rubs, into your daily routine. Physical touch is a powerful way to connect and show affection.

Maya and James's journey reminds us that relationships are a blend of grit and gratitude. By embracing these qualities, couples and families can navigate challenges, deepen their connections, and create a foundation of enduring love and support. Their story, along with the stories of other resilient couples, demonstrates that with commitment and appreciation, any relationship can thrive.

7

Overcoming Adversity with Grit and Gratitude

The story of human achievement is filled with tales of individuals who, in the face of overwhelming adversity, have risen to survive and thrive. These stories are often characterized by two powerful traits: grit and gratitude. This chapter explores real-life stories of comebacks and triumphs, delves into the interplay of grit and gratitude during tough times, and provides practical insights into building resilience through daily practices.

REAL-LIFE STORIES OF COMEBACKS AND TRIUMPHS

THE ARTIST WHO LOST EVERYTHING

Sophie Martinez was a renowned artist whose works were celebrated in galleries worldwide. One night, a fire engulfed her studio, destroying years of her work. She was left with nothing but ashes and a heavy heart. Initially, Sophie was devastated. However, she chose not to wallow in despair. She started anew, using her experience as inspiration. Her new series, "From the Ashes," not only regained her acclaim but also resonated deeply with those who had faced similar adversities. Sophie's story is a testament to how grit—defined as perseverance and passion for long-term goals—can lead to remarkable comebacks.

The Veteran Turned Entrepreneur

James Thompson, a war veteran, returned home with physical injuries and PTSD. He struggled to reintegrate into civilian life. After hitting rock bottom, he channeled his challenges into creating a support network for veterans like himself. He founded "VetConnect," an organization providing veterans job training and mental health support. James's journey from despair to becoming a beacon of hope for others showcases the transformative power of grit and the importance of finding purpose in adversity.

The Single Mother Who Transformed Her Community

Maria Rodriguez, a single mother of three, was laid off from her job at a local factory. Facing financial instability, she started a small business making handmade soaps. Maria's determination and gratitude for her supportive community helped her business flourish despite her initial struggles. Today, her company employs several local women, providing them with stable incomes and transforming the economic landscape of her neighborhood. Maria's story is a powerful example of how grit and gratitude can create lasting positive change.

The Interplay of Grit and Gratitude in Tough Times

Grit and gratitude may seem like an unlikely pair, but their synergy is crucial during challenging times. Grit helps individuals push through obstacles, while gratitude offers a perspective that focuses on what is still good and positive, even in the darkest times.

The Power of Perspective

Consider the story of Lisa, a single mother who lost her job during an economic downturn. With bills and no job prospects, Lisa could have easily given in to despair. Instead, she practiced daily gratitude. Each night, she wrote down three things for which she was thankful. This simple practice shifted her focus from what she had lost to what she still had—her health, her children, and her supportive friends. This perspective fueled her grit, enabling her to pursue job opportunities relentlessly. Eventually,

Lisa found a new job and started a side business that provided additional financial security.

LynnAnn's Dad's Story

Every individual's journey of overcoming adversity is a unique and compelling story. This narrative is a testament to my Dad's remarkable resilience and triumphs, an inspiring and deeply personal story.

My Dad, Hien Khac, at the young age of three years old, experienced a significant loss that his small self probably didn't even comprehend. He lost his father, who was jailed and tortured for teaching history after the Indochina War, a conflict that lasted from 1946 to 1954 and resulted in the division of Vietnam. His mother, a young widow with three young boys, a baby, a three-year-old, my Dad, and a seven-year-old, went to the rice fields to work from dawn to dusk. She left the baby and my Dad in the care of my seven-year-old Uncle, Bac Bang. My Dad told me they were so hungry they went into the jungle and dug up tree roots to chew on. Occasionally, a kind neighbor would share a small rice bowl with them.

There were often floods, and they would sit on the roof of their grass-thatched hut and wait for the water to recede for days. He recalled his baby brother Chu Su crying from hunger, and he and his brother would spoon rice water into his mouth to comfort the baby.

Albeit this incredible suffering, he lived, woke up, found a way to survive, and became a thriving young man. He learned to read and write, and as a teenager, he left his impoverished home to join Catholic seminarian studies and then enlisted in the Army of the Republic of Vietnam as a driver, mechanic, and later signal specialist. He crossed areas of imminent danger and active warfare with a colander on his head and witnessed tragedies beyond comparison. Yet, he preserved made his way to the United States as a refugee. He met his wife, lived, loved, and raised a family.

Each person's experience of adversity is unique, and in Hien Khac's case, it was a profound struggle. Yet, his unwavering faith and gratitude, inspired by his religious beliefs, propelled him from the depths of loss, poverty, and suffering to become an extraordinary father. His story continues to inspire his children, who have gone on to achieve doctoral and master's degrees, serve as civil servants in different abled communities, and join the United States Coast Guard.

Hurricane Katrina Evacuees

My time at the Austin Convention Center and Tony Berger Center, where I worked during the City of Austin's emergency operation disaster response after Hurricane Katrina in August 2005, left a profound mark on me. Every department, including human resources, was called upon to send employees to support the operations. I volunteered to join a team at the evacuation centers, which served as primary shelters for 6000 hurricane evacuees and provided relief and support during the initial stages of the crisis.

One day, I served as a welcome and receiving team member when evacuees arrived at the Austin Convention Center. When the evacuees came off the bus after being rescued from the New Orleans Superdome, their eyes were haunted and glazed. I will never forget the looks on these people's faces. They experienced severe trauma during the hurricane and afterward. The smell was overwhelming because many were still dirty after being rescued from rooftops or walking through flooded places. They had not received clean clothes or running water to clean up. Some mothers and children have not eaten or had access to food for hours or days. The evacuees lost everything and escaped with only the clothes on their backs. It was a horrific situation.

In the Superdome, a last resort shelter, the situation deteriorated quickly for approximately 20,000 to 30,000 people due to needing more necessities like food, water, and sanitation. They had been in the Superdome five days before federal and state authorities evacuated them. As emergency workers, we heard and saw evidence of the horror stories when we supported the evacuees into the centers. The Superdome evacuees experienced chaos and dire issues related to overcrowding, lack of sanitation, and inadequate supplies. Volunteers assisted with medical care, meals, showers, clothing, basic needs distribution, and laundry.

After several days at the centers, mothers, children, and families began to buzz and recover; they checked in to receive housing, employment assistance, and education services. Another day, I worked at the laundry center, and when people received their clean clothes, they expressed appreciation. There were smiles and gratitude for our support. Their grit and gratitude helped them overcome and integrate into the communities.

GRIT, GRATITUDE, AND GRIEF: A JOURNEY OF HEALING

There is no map for navigating the loss of a loved one. Grief strikes with a force that can shatter the foundation of even the strongest among us. While time may help soften the edges of that sorrow, the process of healing is anything but passive. In this space of deep emotional turmoil, cultivating grit and gratitude offers a way forward—two powerful forces that, when combined, can transform how we process loss.

Grit is often spoken of in the context of achieving long-term goals, but when applied to grief, it becomes something more profound. In the face of intense sorrow, grit provides the resilience to stay rooted in life, even when everything feels like it's falling apart. The weight of loss can feel unbearable, and yet, grit is what allows individuals to sit with their pain without being consumed by it. It doesn't promise to take the hurt away, but it offers a kind of emotional armor, helping the grieving person endure and survive the waves of despair.

Perseverance becomes a lifeline in the process. Grief is anything but linear—it ebbs and flows unpredictably, often bringing moments of calm followed by sudden bursts of overwhelming emotion. Yet, in this storm, grit helps individuals continue moving forward. The days can be agonizingly long, filled with an emptiness that feels unshakable, but it is grit that whispers, "Keep going." It allows someone to wake up and face another day, even when their heart feels too heavy to bear.

Life during grief often feels disoriented and chaotic, as though all sense of purpose has been lost. But grit also brings with it the ability to rebuild, little by little. It encourages the setting of small, manageable goals—whether that's getting out of bed, making it through a workday, or finding a meaningful way to honor the memory of the person lost. As goals are met, even the smallest ones, there is a quiet reclaiming of control. In these moments, grit becomes a scaffold, giving individuals a structure to hold onto as they rebuild their lives in the wake of loss.

At the same time, grief has a way of stripping away normal routines and the motivation to care for oneself. Yet, grit also carries within it the seed of self-discipline. Grieving people often neglect their own well-being, retreating from the world. Grit provides the strength to maintain, or even re-establish, habits that keep the body and mind cared for. Exercise, healthy eating, or simply staying connected to loved ones become acts of survival. In these small yet critical practices, grit enables healing, even when it feels like nothing will ever feel "normal" again.

Where grit offers strength, gratitude introduces light. It might seem paradoxical to speak of gratitude during times of grief, but in reality, gratitude is what allows us to find moments of clarity and connection, even amidst the pain. Grief can pull you into darkness, but gratitude invites you to turn your gaze toward the precious memories, the moments shared, and the love that remains. Rather than focusing solely on the absence, gratitude encourages reflection on what was gained from the relationship—a chance to savor the beauty that existed.

In the midst of grief, gratitude can shift focus. Instead of dwelling on the future without your loved one, you begin to appreciate the richness of the past with them. It might be recalling a smile, a shared adventure, or even a difficult time you overcame together. Through this lens, their memory becomes something to cherish, rather than just a source of pain. You start to see how their presence, no matter how brief, shaped your life in meaningful ways.

More importantly, gratitude allows a deep appreciation for the time spent with your loved one. There is no pretending the pain of loss isn't real, but gratitude makes room for the acknowledgement that the time shared was a gift. Every moment, every conversation, every memory becomes a treasure that helps reframe the grief as part of a larger story—one filled with love, connection, and shared experiences.

Gratitude also fosters a continued sense of connection, even after the person is gone. It nurtures the feeling that the relationship hasn't ended; it has transformed. In the act of remembering and appreciating, we find ways to stay close to those we've lost. Gratitude turns memories into something active, something that keeps their spirit alive within us.

When grit and gratitude are intertwined, something even more powerful happens. Together, they allow for what's known as post-traumatic growth—when a person emerges from grief not just surviving, but transformed by the experience. With grit, they've built the resilience to face loss head-on; with gratitude, they've found ways to honor that loss by holding on to what's meaningful. This combination leads to a deeper sense of purpose, where the individual can find meaning in the midst of pain.

As the grieving process unfolds, there's often a natural desire to honor the memory of the loved one. In this space, grit and gratitude can come together to inspire acts of kindness, charity, or creative expression in their name. Whether it's starting a foundation, writing a memoir, or simply living a life that reflects the values of the person lost, these actions become a way to turn grief into something life-affirming. In this way, loss becomes a catalyst for growth, and the memory of the loved one lives on in acts of love and generosity.

Grief is a journey, one that looks different for everyone. Grit and gratitude don't erase the pain or provide easy answers, but they offer tools for navigating the darkness. With grit, we find the strength to keep moving forward; with gratitude, we find light to guide our way. Together, they create a path toward healing, where the memory of those we've lost becomes a source of strength, not sorrow.

SCHOLARLY INSIGHT

Research by psychologist Angela Duckworth has extensively explored the concept of grit. In her seminal book, *Grit: The Power of Passion and Perseverance*, Duckworth defines grit as a combination of passion and perseverance for long-term goals. Her studies have shown that grit significantly predicts success in various domains, from academic achievement to personal development (Duckworth, 2016). Furthermore, studies have shown that gratitude can enhance well-being and resilience. Emmons and McCullough (2003) found that individuals who regularly practiced gratitude reported higher levels of positive emotions, life satisfaction, and lower levels of depression and stress.

BUILDING RESILIENCE THROUGH DAILY PRACTICES

Building resilience is not an overnight process; it involves daily practices that strengthen mental and emotional fortitude.

MINDFULNESS AND MEDITATION

Mindfulness and meditation are powerful tools for cultivating resilience. They help individuals stay present and manage stress effectively. By setting aside just 10 minutes daily for mindfulness practice, individuals can significantly enhance their emotional resilience, making it easier to navigate life's challenges with a clear and focused mind. A study by Davidson et al. (2003) showed that mindfulness meditation can lead to brain function changes associated with improved emotional regulation and stress management.

PHYSICAL ACTIVITY

Regular physical activity is another crucial component of resilience. Exercise releases endorphins, which help improve mood and reduce stress. Whether it's a morning run, a yoga session, or a simple walk in the park, staying active is essential for maintaining both physical and mental health.

Research by Babyak et al. (2000) found that exercise was as effective as medication in treating major depression, highlighting its importance for mental well-being.

EXPRESSING GRATITUDE

Gratitude practices, such as keeping a gratitude journal or expressing appreciation to others, can significantly boost emotional resilience. By regularly acknowledging the positive aspects of life, individuals can foster a sense of contentment and well-being, even in difficult times. A study by Seligman, Steen, Park, and Peterson (2005) demonstrated that gratitude interventions could enhance well-being and decrease depressive symptoms.

INSPIRATIONAL EXAMPLES AND LESSONS LEARNED

THE MARATHON RUNNER

John Harrison was an avid marathon runner who was diagnosed with a severe heart condition. Doctors told him he would never run again. Instead of giving up, John focused on what he could still do. He began walking, then jogging, and eventually, running short distances. With each step, he expressed gratitude for his body's ability to heal and adapt. Years later, John completed a marathon, proving that determination and gratitude can defy even the most daunting odds.

THE TEACHER WHO TRANSFORMED LIVES

Sarah Green, a high school teacher in a low-income neighborhood, faced daily challenges with her students, many of whom struggled with personal and academic issues. Rather than becoming disheartened, Sarah approached each day with gratitude for the opportunity to make a difference. Her grit in developing creative teaching methods and her gratitude for the small victories significantly improved her students' performance and well-being. Sarah's story highlights how a positive attitude and relentless effort can create ripples of change in the community.

The Scientist Who Revolutionized Medicine

Dr. Jane Mitchell faced numerous rejections and setbacks in her quest to develop a groundbreaking cancer treatment. Despite the challenges, she remained steadfast in her research, driven by a deep purpose and gratitude for every small breakthrough. Her perseverance paid off when her treatment received approval, saving countless lives. Dr. Mitchell's journey exemplifies how grit and gratitude can lead to revolutionary advancements in science and medicine.

Overcoming adversity requires a delicate balance of grit and gratitude. Through real-life stories and practical daily practices, this chapter has illustrated how these traits can lead to extraordinary comebacks and triumphs. By embracing resilience and maintaining a grateful perspective, we can survive the challenges life throws our way and emerge stronger and more fulfilled. Remember, it's not just about getting through tough times; it's about growing through them.

8

The Role of Grit and Gratitude in Personal Growth

CONTINUOUS SELF-IMPROVEMENT AND LIFELONG LEARNING

The journey of personal growth is not a destination but a perpetual path. Continuous self-improvement and lifelong learning form the bedrock of this journey. Grit and gratitude, though seemingly simple concepts, are the pillars that sustain and elevate our progress.

In her seminal work on grit, Angela Duckworth defines it as "passion and perseverance for long-term goals" (Duckworth, 2016). Grit is the determination that keeps you moving forward despite the steep inclines, the rocky paths, and the exhaustion. The internal fire propels you to push past obstacles and continue your ascent. On the other hand, lifelong learning is akin to gathering tools and knowledge along the way, ensuring you are better equipped for the journey. Each lesson learned and skill acquired becomes a foothold, making the climb more manageable and the summit closer with every step.

Take, for instance, the story of Ben, a software developer who decided to learn a new programming language each year. His commitment to continuous self-improvement allowed him to stay ahead in his field, confidently tackling complex projects. Ben's grit enabled him to persist through the initial confusion and frustration that often accompanies learning something new. His gratitude, meanwhile, kept his grounded, appreciating the progress he made and the support he received from his peers.

Similarly, consider Nina, a teacher dedicated to learning new teaching methodologies. Her passion for education drove her to attend workshops, enroll in online courses, and collaborate with other educators. Nina's grit enabled her to persist even when implementing new strategies was challenging, and her gratitude helped her appreciate her positive impact on her students' lives.

BALANCING AMBITION WITH CONTENTMENT

The drive to achieve more can be a double-edged sword. On one hand, ambition fuels progress, pushing us to set higher goals and reach new heights. On the other hand, unchecked ambition can lead to burnout and dissatisfaction. The key lies in balancing ambition with contentment.

Grit without gratitude can turn ambition into a relentless pursuit, leaving one feeling empty despite numerous achievements. Conversely, gratitude without grit may lead to complacency, stalling personal growth. The harmony between the two creates a powerful dynamic where ambition is tempered with appreciation, fostering both achievement and fulfillment.

Consider Ellie, a marketing executive with a fast-paced career. Her ambition led her to constantly seek promotions and new challenges, leaving her feeling dissatisfied. By integrating gratitude into her daily routine—taking time to reflect on her accomplishments and appreciate the present—Ellie found a balance. Her grit continued to drive her forward, but her gratitude allowed her to savor the journey, not just the destination.

In another example, Alecia, a competitive athlete, learned to balance her intense training with moments of mindfulness and reflection. Her ambition pushed her to set and achieve new records. Still, her practice of gratitude—acknowledging her body's capabilities and her team's support— kept her mentally and emotionally balanced.

SETTING AND ACHIEVING PERSONAL GOALS

Setting personal goals is an essential aspect of personal growth. It gives direction to our efforts and a sense of purpose. However, achieving these goals requires more than determination; it requires a strategic approach intertwined with resilience and appreciation.

Start with clarity. Define what you want to achieve and why it matters to you. This clarity fuels your grit, compelling you to persevere when challenges arise. Break down your goals into smaller, manageable tasks. This makes the process less daunting and allows for frequent moments of achievement, which bolsters your resolve.

Edwin Locke and Gary Latham's Goal-Setting Theory highlights the importance of setting clear, challenging goals to enhance performance (Locke & Latham, 2002). Goals give direction and purpose to our efforts, motivating us to persist even in the face of adversity.

Emily, a freelance writer, wanted to publish her own book. She set specific milestones—completing a chapter each month, seeking feedback from peers, and revising her drafts. Her grit kept her writing through late nights and early mornings, while her gratitude kept her motivated by celebrating small victories, like positive feedback or a particularly well-written passage.

Likewise, John, described earlier in this book, set a goal to launch his start-up. He divided his goal into achievable steps—market research, securing funding, developing a prototype, and marketing. His grit helped him navigate setbacks and challenges, while his gratitude ensured he recognized and celebrated each milestone, keeping his motivation high.

REFLECTIVE PRACTICES FOR ONGOING DEVELOPMENT

Reflective practices are vital for ongoing personal development. They provide a space to pause, assess progress, and recalibrate goals if necessary. Grit and gratitude play significant roles in these practices.

Reflection involves honest self-assessment, recognizing both achievements and areas for improvement. It requires the grit to confront uncomfortable truths and the gratitude to appreciate how far you've come. Journaling, meditation, and regular feedback sessions are effective reflective practices.

Lucas, an entrepreneur, dedicated weekly time to reflect on his business and personal growth. He journaled about his successes and setbacks, always seeking lessons from his experiences. This practice honed his resilience as he learned to navigate failures with a growth mindset. His gratitude practice, listing three things he was thankful for daily, kept him positive and focused on the bigger picture.

Another effective practice is seeking mentorship. A young professional, Anna regularly met with her mentor to discuss her career progress. These sessions allowed her to reflect on her goals, receive constructive feedback, and gain new perspectives. Her mentor encouraged her to embrace grit and gratitude, helping her navigate her career path with resilience and appreciation.

As a graduate student, JoAnn unplugged from school, her life as a mom, and her spouse to take regular hikes and be in nature to clear space for reflection. The practice of unplugging everything and connecting with nature helped her reflect on how grit and gratitude.

The interplay between grit and gratitude is crucial in personal growth. Continuous self-improvement and lifelong learning require the determination to push forward and the humility to keep learning. Balancing ambition with contentment ensures that pursuing goals does not overshadow the joy of the journey. Setting and achieving personal goals become more fulfilling when driven by both passion and appreciation. Finally, reflective practices provide the necessary checkpoints to stay on course and grow consistently.

Embracing grit and gratitude transforms personal growth from a daunting climb into a rewarding adventure. It's about striving to be better while cherishing the progress made, pushing through challenges while appreciating the lessons learned, and ultimately, achieving goals with a deep sense of fulfillment.

The role of grit and gratitude in personal growth is like that of a compass and a map. Grit guides you forward, ensuring you never lose your way despite the difficulties, while gratitude helps you appreciate the landscape, finding joy and meaning in every step. Together, they create a balanced, fulfilling journey of self-improvement and lifelong learning.

9

Grit and Gratitude in Health and Wellbeing

Two powerful traits stand out in the journey toward a healthier and more fulfilling life: grit and gratitude. This chapter delves into the profound impact of these qualities on physical health, mental well-being, and overall life satisfaction. Through stories of healing and recovery, we explore how integrating grit and gratitude into a holistic wellness plan can lead to transformative changes.

PHYSICAL HEALTH BENEFITS OF GRIT AND GRATITUDE

Grit, often described as perseverance and passion for long-term goals, has been linked to numerous physical health benefits. Individuals who exhibit high levels of grit tend to maintain healthier lifestyles. Despite setbacks, they are more likely to engage in regular physical activity, adhere to medical advice, and pursue long-term health goals. This relentless commitment to health can lower rates of chronic illnesses, such as heart disease and diabetes, and contribute to a longer lifespan.

On the other hand, gratitude, the quality of being thankful and showing appreciation, has a more immediate and soothing impact on the body. Research has shown that practicing gratitude can improve sleep quality, lower blood pressure, and enhanced immune function. The simple act of acknowledging and appreciating the good in one's life can reduce stress hormones like cortisol, lowering the risk of stress-related ailments.

In a study published in the journal *Personality and Individual Differences*, researchers found that individuals who regularly practiced gratitude had better heart health, measured by reduced blood pressure and lower levels of inflammatory biomarkers. These individuals also reported fewer aches and pains and were more likely to take care of their health by exercising regularly and attending regular check-ups. Grit, meanwhile, helps sustain these healthy habits over the long term, fostering an environment where physical health can thrive.

MENTAL HEALTH AND EMOTIONAL STABILITY

The mental health benefits of grit and gratitude are equally compelling. Gritty individuals are often more resilient in the face of adversity. Their ability to persist through challenges can buffer against anxiety and depression, fostering a sense of purpose and direction. This resilience is not just about enduring hardship but also about bouncing back and growing stronger from it.

A study from the *Journal of Personality and Social Psychology* demonstrated that grit predicts success and well-being over and above intelligence and talent. Gritty individuals often have a growth mindset, viewing challenges as opportunities for development rather than insurmountable obstacles. This perspective is crucial for mental health, as it encourages perseverance and resilience in the face of difficulties.

Gratitude, focusing on positive reflection, can shift one's mindset from negative rumination to positive appreciation. Regularly practicing gratitude has been shown to increase happiness and life satisfaction levels while decreasing symptoms of depression. By cultivating an attitude of gratitude, individuals can enhance their emotional stability, making them less susceptible to mood swings and more capable of maintaining a positive outlook.

In clinical settings, gratitude interventions have been used to treat various psychological issues. For example, patients with chronic pain who practiced gratitude reported significant reductions in perceived pain and depressive symptoms. The practice of gratitude can rewire the brain to recognize and appreciate the positive aspects of life, even amid hardship.

STORIES OF HEALING AND RECOVERY

Consider the story of Emma, a young woman diagnosed with a chronic illness that left her debilitated and despondent. Initially overwhelmed by her condition, Emma decided to embrace grit. She set small, achievable goals, such as walking a few extra steps daily or practicing yoga for ten minutes. Her unwavering determination gradually improved her physical strength and mobility. Simultaneously, Emma kept a gratitude journal, noting three things she was thankful for each day, no matter how small. This practice shifted her focus from her pain to the positive aspects of her life, enhancing her emotional resilience.

Then there's the tale of James, a veteran who struggled with post-traumatic stress disorder (PTSD). Traditional therapies helped, but what truly made a difference was his adoption of a gratitude practice. By actively seeking and expressing gratitude, James found a way to reconnect with the world around him. Coupled with his gritty determination to regain control over his life, he experienced significant improvements in his mental health. James' story is a testament to the healing power of combining grit and gratitude.

Let's also look at the story of Sofia, an entrepreneur who faced a major business failure. The collapse of her business was a devastating blow, affecting her financial stability and mental health. Instead of succumbing to despair, Sofia harnessed her grit to rebuild her life. She sought new opportunities, networked tirelessly, and learned from her past mistakes. Alongside her gritty efforts, she began practicing daily gratitude, which helped her stay positive and recognize the support she received from her friends and family. This combination of grit and gratitude helped Sofia recover and led to the creation of a new, even more successful business venture.

Lee, a civil servant, was a victim of a bicycle hit-and-run and robbery during a crime spree. He suffered life-threatening head injuries, but he persevered and continued his long recovery through surgeries and therapy to serve as an advocate for individuals with disabilities. His grit, commitment to service, and gratitude for his constituents helped him survive the violent acts and overcome his injuries.

INTEGRATING GRIT AND GRATITUDE INTO A HOLISTIC WELLNESS PLAN

To harness the benefits of grit and gratitude, it's essential to integrate these traits into a comprehensive wellness plan. Here's how you can start:

1. **Set Clear, Achievable Goals:** Define what you want to achieve regarding physical health and emotional well-being. Break down these goals into manageable steps and celebrate small victories along the way.

2. **Develop a Routine:** Consistency is key. Establish daily habits that promote both physical activity and moments of reflection. This might include regular exercise, mindfulness practices, or keeping a gratitude journal.

3. **Cultivate Resilience:** When faced with setbacks, remind yourself of your long-term goals and the progress you've made. Embrace challenges as opportunities to grow and strengthen your grit.

4. **Practice Daily Gratitude:** Make it a habit to reflect on the positive aspects of your day. Write down three things you are grateful for each evening, and share your gratitude with others to deepen its impact.

5. **Seek Support:** Surround yourself with a supportive community that encourages your efforts and shares in your journey. Whether through friends, family, or support groups, connection plays a vital role in maintaining motivation and emotional health.

6. **Mind-Body Practices:** Incorporate practices that align your physical and mental health, such as yoga, tai chi, or meditation. These activities can enhance both your grit by promoting discipline and your gratitude by fostering mindfulness.

7. **Mindful Reflection:** At the end of each week, take some time to reflect on your achievements and the things you are grateful for. This practice can help reinforce your commitment to your goals and maintain a positive outlook.

8. **Balanced Nutrition:** A healthy diet can significantly impact your physical and mental health. Grit can help you stick to nutritional goals, while gratitude for the food you eat can enhance your enjoyment and mindfulness around meals.

9. **Sleep Hygiene:** Prioritize good sleep habits. Grit can help you maintain a consistent sleep schedule, and gratitude practices before bed can improve sleep quality by reducing stress and promoting relaxation.

10. **Regular Check-ups:** Make regular appointments with healthcare providers to monitor and maintain your health. Use your grit to keep these appointments on schedule, and express gratitude for the care and support you receive.

You can create a robust framework for enduring health and well-being by embedding grit and gratitude into your daily life. The stories of Emma, James, and Sofia illustrate that even in the face of significant challenges, these traits can lead to profound healing and transformation. Embrace the power of grit and gratitude, and watch as they guide you towards a healthier, more fulfilling life.

GRIT AND GRATITUDE IN ACKNOWLEDGING SOCIAL ADVANTAGES AND BIASES

In the intricate web of society, we are born into positions that can either propel us forward or weigh us down. These positions are often determined by invisible forces tied to our race, gender, socioeconomic status, education, physical ability, sexual orientation, and even age. These forces grant some individuals an inherent advantage, a head start in a race they may not even realize they are running. Others are burdened with obstacles that make the finish line seem distant, if not unreachable. These social advantages shape our access to resources, opportunities, and power, often reinforcing inequities and perpetuating a cycle of privilege for some while marginalizing others.

At the core of these advantages lie biases—deep-seated notions that we carry, whether consciously or unconsciously, that influence how we perceive and treat others. These biases can manifest in many ways:

- **Implicit Bias:** The hidden, unconscious stereotypes we hold that subtly influence our judgments and actions without our awareness.
- **Explicit Bias:** The overt prejudices we consciously harbor and may even express openly.
- **Confirmation Bias:** The tendency to seek out and favor information that supports our pre-existing beliefs, while ignoring or downplaying evidence that contradicts them.
- **Affinity Bias:** The preference for those who are similar to ourselves, whether in appearance, background, or belief.

These biases serve as filters through which we view the world, often reinforcing the advantages we possess and perpetuating inequalities by limiting opportunities for those who differ from us. If left unexamined, they fuel a system where certain groups continuously benefit at the expense of others.

The path to dismantling these biases and confronting our social advantages is neither easy nor comfortable. It requires grit—the relentless perseverance to face difficult truths—and gratitude, the deep appreciation for the journey and the lessons learned along the way. Together, grit and gratitude form a powerful framework for self-reflection, growth, and action.

THE ROLE OF GRIT: RESILIENCE IN DISCOMFORT

Grit is often defined as the courage and resolve to persevere in the face of challenges. In the context of acknowledging social advantages and biases, it demands something deeper—a courageous self-reflection. It takes grit to confront the reality of our own privilege or to admit that we have unconsciously benefited from systems that disadvantage others.

Courageous Self-Reflection: Acknowledging social advantages requires us to look inward and confront uncomfortable truths about how our identity has shaped our experiences. Grit gives us the strength to face this head-on, without retreating into defensiveness or denial.

Resilience in Discomfort: The process of understanding our biases and privileges is rarely easy. It can bring feelings of guilt, shame, or discomfort. Grit helps us sit with these emotions, building resilience as we work through them rather than turning away.

Perseverance in Learning: Biases are not easily unlearned. They are deeply ingrained in our thought patterns, often shaped by years of cultural conditioning. Grit fuels a growth mindset, pushing us to keep learning and evolving, even when the work feels exhausting or overwhelming.

Self-Discipline in Self-Awareness: Grit is about consistency. It's about making a commitment to regularly reflect on our thoughts, actions, and behaviors, recognizing where biases might be influencing our decisions, and challenging ourselves to do better each day.

THE POWER OF GRATITUDE: HUMILITY AND OPENNESS

While grit keeps us moving forward, gratitude softens the edges of the journey. It brings a sense of humility, helping us recognize the invisible scaffolding that has supported us along the way.

Appreciation for Diverse Perspectives: Gratitude shifts our focus from self-centered perspectives to a broader, more inclusive view. It encourages us to appreciate the richness that diversity brings to our lives, fostering empathy and a deeper understanding of those whose experiences differ from our own.

Recognition of Social Advantages: When we practice gratitude, we become more aware of the privileges we may have taken for granted. This recognition is not meant to induce guilt but rather to cultivate a sense of responsibility and awareness. Gratitude allows us to appreciate the advantages we've had and motivates us to use them in ways that benefit others.

Humility: Gratitude naturally breeds humility. It reminds us that no matter how hard we have worked or how much we have achieved, many factors beyond our control have contributed to our success. This humility opens the door to acknowledging our limitations and biases without feeling personally attacked or diminished.

Openness to Feedback: A mindset of gratitude makes us more receptive to constructive criticism. When we are grateful, we see feedback not as a personal affront, but as an opportunity for growth. This openness is crucial when confronting our biases, as it allows us to listen, learn, and adjust our behavior in meaningful ways.

THE SYNERGY OF GRIT AND GRATITUDE: A PATH TO GROWTH

When combined, grit and gratitude create a balanced approach to understanding our social advantages and biases—one that is grounded in both courage and humility.

Courageous Gratitude: Practicing gratitude with grit means approaching our biases with both humility and resilience. It enables us to recognize our privilege without succumbing to guilt, and to acknowledge our biases without defensiveness. This combination allows us to move forward with both strength and compassion.

Self-Awareness and Growth: Grit pushes us to keep learning, while gratitude encourages reflection and appreciation. Together, they foster a deeper self-awareness, allowing us to grow in our understanding of how our social advantages and biases shape our interactions with the world.

Empathy and Compassion: As we develop grit and gratitude, we become more empathetic to the struggles of marginalized groups. We begin to see the world through a more compassionate lens, understanding that not everyone starts from the same place or has access to the same resources. This empathy fuels our desire to create a more equitable and inclusive society.

Accountability and Action: Ultimately, the goal of grit and gratitude is not just self-awareness, but action. Grit gives us the strength to take responsibility for our biases and privileges, while gratitude inspires us to use our advantages for the greater good. Together, they motivate us to engage in meaningful change, whether through advocacy, allyship, or direct action.

By embracing both grit and gratitude, we embark on a journey toward greater self-awareness, empathy, and social responsibility. We learn to navigate the complexities of privilege and bias with both courage and humility, and in doing so, contribute to a more just and compassionate world.

10

The Global Impact of Grit and Gratitude

In the tapestry of human history, two powerful threads often interwoven into the fabric of our most outstanding achievements are grit and gratitude. Often seen as personal virtues, these traits extend far beyond the individual. They shape communities, influence societies, and have the potential to drive global change.

THE POWER OF GRIT AND GRATITUDE IN SHAPING SOCIETIES

Grit, the relentless pursuit of goals in the face of obstacles, has been a cornerstone in developing resilient communities. Societies embody this trait push through adversity, turning challenges into opportunities for growth. Meanwhile, gratitude fosters a sense of belonging and mutual respect, essential components for the cohesion of any community.

Consider the reconstruction of Europe after World War II. The continent lay in ruins, economies were shattered, and millions were displaced. Yet, through collective grit, European nations rebuilt their cities, economies, and societies. The Marshall Plan, an American initiative to aid Western Europe, exemplified gratitude on a global scale. The United States, recognizing the importance of a stable Europe for world peace, extended a helping hand, fostering recovery and a lasting bond of cooperation and trust.

HISTORICAL EXAMPLES OF COLLECTIVE GRIT AND GRATITUDE

History is replete with examples of societies that have harnessed these traits to effect monumental change. During the Great Depression, the grit of the American people was palpable. Despite widespread poverty and unemployment, communities came together, supported each other, and found ways to survive and eventually thrive. The New Deal, with its focus on job creation and social safety nets, was a manifestation of governmental gratitude towards its citizens, acknowledging their struggles and striving to provide relief and opportunities.

Another powerful example is the Indian independence movement. Under British colonial rule, India faced economic exploitation and social oppression. However, India eventually gained its freedom through the unwavering grit of its leaders and citizens, exemplified by Mahatma Gandhi's non-violent resistance. The gratitude of the Indian people towards their leaders and the international support they received played a crucial role in sustaining their struggle.

In more recent times, the global response to the COVID-19 pandemic has demonstrated the power of collective grit and gratitude. crisis during an unprecedented crisis. At the same time, acts of gratitude, from clapping for healthcare workers to international cooperation on vaccine distribution, highlighted the importance of recognizing and appreciating each other's efforts.

ENCOURAGING A GLOBAL MOVEMENT

In today's interconnected world, the principles of grit and gratitude can catalyze a global movement. Social media platforms, international organizations, and cross-border collaborations provide unprecedented opportunities to spread these values.

Initiatives like the Global Citizen movement highlight how collective efforts can address global challenges. By encouraging individuals to take action on issues like poverty, climate change, and inequality, Global Citizen harnesses the grit of millions around the world. Simultaneously, celebrating achievements and milestones fosters a culture of gratitude, recognizing the contributions of those who strive for a better world.

Educational programs focusing on these values can also play a pivotal role. Teaching children the importance of perseverance and the power of gratitude can create a generation ready to tackle global issues with resilience and empathy. Schools that incorporate service learning, where students engage in community service, help inculcate these traits from a young age.

PRACTICAL STEPS TO FOSTER GRIT AND GRATITUDE GLOBALLY

1. **Promote Stories of Resilience:** Media and educational institutions can highlight stories of individuals and communities demonstrating exceptional grit and gratitude. Documentaries, books, and articles that showcase these values can inspire others to follow suit.

2. **Create Platforms for Recognition:** Establishing awards and recognition programs for acts of grit and gratitude can motivate individuals and groups to pursue these values. Platforms like the Nobel Peace Prize and the United Nations recognitions can be powerful examples.

3. **Encourage Cross-Cultural Exchange:** International exchange programs can foster understanding and appreciation between cultures, highlighting the universal nature of grit and gratitude. These exchanges can build empathy and global solidarity.

4. **Support Grassroots Movements:** Grassroots initiatives that embody grit and gratitude should receive support from governments, NGOs, and the private sector. Providing resources and platforms for these movements can amplify their impact.

5. **Integrate Values into Corporate Culture:** Businesses can incorporate grit and gratitude into corporate social responsibility (CSR) initiatives. Companies that value perseverance and recognize their employees' and communities' contributions can drive positive social change.

THE FUTURE OF A WORLD EMBRACING GRIT AND GRATITUDE

Imagine a world where nations collaborate with the same determination and mutual respect seen in small, tight-knit communities. A world where the grit to overcome challenges is matched by gratitude for the support and contributions of others.

Such a world would likely reduce conflicts, as nations and peoples would focus on common goals rather than differences. International relations would be strengthened by mutual respect and acknowledgment of each other's efforts. Global issues like climate change, poverty, and health crises would be tackled with a united front, combining resilience and appreciation for collective action.

Technological advancements can also foster these values. If used responsibly, social media platforms can spread messages of resilience and gratitude, encouraging positive behavior on a global scale. Virtual reality (VR) experiences can allow individuals to step into the shoes of others, building empathy and understanding.

In politics, leaders who exemplify grit and gratitude can inspire their nations to adopt these values. Policies that support social equity, environmental sustainability, and international cooperation can reflect a commitment to these principles.

As we move forward, integrating grit and gratitude into our global consciousness could transform how we address challenges and celebrate successes. By embracing these principles, we can build a future that is not only resilient but also deeply connected by a shared sense of purpose and appreciation.

Grit and gratitude are more than just personal virtues; they are potent forces that can shape the destiny of communities, nations, and the world. We can encourage a global movement towards a more resilient, compassionate, and united future by fostering these traits.

Conclusion -
Your Comeback Story

REFLECTING ON PERSONAL GROWTH THROUGHOUT THE BOOK

As we reach the final chapter of this journey, it's time to reflect on the path we've walked together. The chapters of this book have been designed to guide you through the labyrinth of challenges, offering tools, strategies, and insights to help you overcome obstacles and rediscover your inner strength. Each story, each lesson, and each piece of advice has been curated with one goal: to empower you to craft your own comeback story.

Think back to where you started. Perhaps you felt lost, overwhelmed, or unsure of your next steps. Maybe you were grappling with feelings of inadequacy, isolation, or fear. As you moved through the chapters, you learned to confront these emotions head-on, transforming them into stepping stones to personal growth. You discovered the power of resilience, the importance of self-compassion, and the undeniable strength of embracing your vulnerabilities.

Remember the exercises we practiced together—the moments of introspection that allowed you to delve deep into your psyche, unearthing hidden strengths and untapped potential. Recall the stories of those who have faced similar struggles and emerged stronger, their experiences serving as beacons of hope and inspiration. Through their journeys, you saw that no setback is insurmountable, no obstacle too significant to overcome.

Consider the transformative power of mindfulness we discussed. It allows you to stay present in the moment, reducing stress and increasing your capacity to deal with adversity. Consider the importance of setting boundaries, as explored in our chapter on self-care, and how this has empowered you to protect your time and energy, leading to a more balanced and fulfilling life.

Reflect on the importance of community and connection. We examined how building a supportive network can be a critical buffer against life's challenges. The strength you've gained from your relationships with others has likely reinforced your sense of belonging and reduced feelings of loneliness and isolation.

ENCOURAGEMENT AND FINAL THOUGHTS

As you stand at the precipice of your comeback story, know that the journey doesn't end here. Life is a continuous series of peaks and valleys, victories and setbacks. But with your acquired tools, you are better equipped to navigate these fluctuations. You have learned that growth is not linear, and setbacks are not failures but opportunities for learning and development.

Believe in your capacity for change. Embrace the discomfort that comes with growth, for it is in these moments of challenge that true transformation occurs. Trust in your ability to adapt, to rise above adversity, and to create a life that reflects your values, passions, and dreams.

Remember, setbacks are a natural part of any journey. It's how you respond to these setbacks that define your character and shape your future. Every challenge you've faced and overcome has made you stronger, more resilient, and more capable of facing whatever comes next.

CALL TO ACTION: EMBRACE GRIT AND GRATITUDE IN YOUR OWN LIFE

Now, we call upon you to take action. Embrace grit and gratitude in your daily life. Grit will give you the tenacity to keep pushing forward, even when the road is tough. It will remind you that persistence, more than talent or luck, leads to success. Cultivate a mindset of resilience, viewing challenges as opportunities to grow stronger and wiser.

Gratitude, on the other hand, will keep you grounded. It will remind you of the beauty and goodness that exist even in the darkest of times. Make it a habit to reflect on what you are thankful for each day, no matter how small. Gratitude will open your heart and mind to the abundance that surrounds you, fostering a sense of contentment and peace.

Together, grit and gratitude form a powerful combination, enabling you to face life's challenges with strength and grace. They will guide you through the toughest times and illuminate your path to a brighter future.

To embrace grit, start by setting small, manageable goals that lead towards your larger aspirations. Break down daunting tasks into smaller, actionable steps, and celebrate each milestone you achieve along the way. Surround yourself with individuals who inspire you and push you to be your best self. Remember, grit is not about never failing—it's about never giving up.

Gratitude can be cultivated through simple daily practices. Keep a gratitude journal where you write down three things you are grateful for each day. Share your appreciation with others, whether through a kind word, a thank-you note, or a simple act of kindness. By consistently focusing on the positive aspects of your life, you'll find that gratitude becomes a natural part of your mindset, enriching your life and the lives of those around you.

RESOURCES FOR FURTHER PRACTICE, READING AND SUPPORT

Your journey of personal growth and resilience doesn't have to end with this book. Countless resources are available to support you as you continue to evolve and thrive.

Here are a few recommendations:

ACTIVITY

Write your comeback story. Documenting your journey is a way to connect to your comeback story through grit and gratitude. Write down the situation, your grit and gratitude, your actions, and the results. Keep a journal of your comeback stories.

BOOKS

1. "Grit: The Power of Passion and Perseverance"* by Angela Duckworth
2. "The Gifts of Imperfection"* by Brené Brown
3. "Man's Search for Meaning"* by Viktor E. Frankl
4. "Atomic Habits: An Easy & Proven Way to Build Good Habits & Break Bad Ones"* by James Clear
5. "The Power of Now: A Guide to Spiritual Enlightenment"* by Eckhart Tolle
6. "Daring Greatly: How the Courage to Be Vulnerable Transforms the Way We Live, Love, Parent, and Lead"* by Brené Brown

WEBSITES AND BLOGS:

1. Positive Psychology: www.positivepsychology.com
2. Tiny Buddha: www.tinybuddha.com
3. Mindful: www.mindful.org
4. Greater Good Science Center: www.greatergood.berkeley.edu

SUPPORT GROUPS AND COMMUNITIES:

1. Meetup: www.meetup.com (search for support groups in your area)
2. The Mighty: www.themighty.com (a supportive online community)
3. BetterUp Coaching: www.betterup.com (a supportive online coaching community)
4. Local community centers and organizations often offer support groups and resources.

PODCASTS:

1. Huberman Lab
2. The Tony Robbins Podcast
3. The Happiness Lab with Dr. Laurie Santos
4. The Art of Happiness with Arthur Brooks
5. The Daily Stoic Podcast

Remember, your comeback story is a testament to your strength, resilience, and unwavering spirit. Keep moving forward, embrace every challenge, and continue to write the narrative of your incredible journey. Your story is far from over—it is just beginning. With each step you take, you are transforming your life and inspiring those around you to do the same. So, go forth with grit and gratitude, and let your comeback story shine brightly for all to see.

References

Babyak, M., Blumenthal, J. A., Herman, S., Khatri, P., Doraiswamy, M., Moore, K., ... & Krishnan, K. R. (2000). Exercise treatment for major depression: Maintenance of therapeutic benefit at 10 months. *Psychosomatic Medicine, 62*(5), 633-638.

Davidson, R. J., Kabat-Zinn, J., Schumacher, J., Rosenkranz, M., Muller, D., Santorelli, S. F., ... & Sheridan, J. F. (2003). Alterations in brain and immune function produced by mindfulness meditation. *Psychosomatic Medicine, 65*(4), 564-570.

Duckworth, A. (2016). *Grit: The Power of Passion and Perseverance*. Scribner.

Emmons, R. A., & McCullough, M. E. (2003). Counting blessings versus burdens: An experimental investigation of gratitude and subjective well-being in daily life. *Journal of Personality and Social Psychology, 84*(2), 377-389.

Locke, E. A., & Latham, G. P. (2002). Building a practically useful theory of goal setting and task motivation: A 35-year odyssey. *American Psychologist, 57*(9), 705-717.

Seligman, M. E., Steen, T. A., Park, N., & Peterson, C. (2005). Positive psychology progress: Empirical validation of interventions. *American Psychologist, 60*(5), 410-421.

www.ingramcontent.com/pod-product-compliance
Lightning Source LLC
Chambersburg PA
CBHW072012150726
47999CB00002B/613